I0214599

Boundaries and Frontiers in Medieval Muslim Geography

TRANSACTIONS

of the

American Philosophical Society

Held at Philadelphia for Promoting Useful Knowledge

VOLUME 85, Part 6, 1995

Boundaries and Frontiers in Medieval Muslim Geography

RALPH W. BRAUER

Institute for Research on the
Interaction of Science and Culture
Wilmington, NC 28401

THE AMERICAN PHILOSOPHICAL SOCIETY

Independence Square, Philadelphia

1995

Copyright © 1995 by The American Philosophical Society
All rights reserved. Reproduction in any media is restricted.

This work was supported in part by grants from
the Max and Victoria Dreyfus Foundation
and the Foundation for the Carolinas

Library of Congress Catalog
Card Number: 94-78513
International Standard Book Number 0-87169-856-0
US ISSN 0065-9746

TABLE OF CONTENTS

SECTION 1

The Geographical Concepts

It has been pointed out that the concept of the state is linked to a perception of its territoriality.[1] Therefore, the character of the boundaries that confine a given state reflect important aspects of the view taken by the inhabitants of the nature of their polity. While translating al-Idrisi's "Book of Roger"–the "Kitāb nuzha 'l-muštāq fi 'ktirāq al-afāq"–his great 'Opus Geographicum,' I failed to encounter any reference to boundaries between various political or ethnographic units in either the text of this work or the maps accompanying it. In view of the importance of boundary concepts, this observation seemed worthy of further inquiry to determine whether it might represent a mere idiosyncrasy of this one author, or prove to be a reflection of a more general characteristic of the geographic concepts current in the Arabo-Islamic civilization.

This monograph presents the relevant data from Arabo-Islamic scholars, relating them to the experiences of observers other than the scholar-geographers, testing them by reference to a second Islamicized population, and finally defining some of the questions raised by the data.

Boundaries in Arabo-Islamic Cartography

The earliest known map by Muslim scholars, al-Ma'mūn's world map of the beginning of the ninth century, unfortunately is lost. While its general outlines can be reconstructed with some confidence on the basis of al-Ḵwarizmī's geography treatise,[2] only a few small bits of actual cartography attributed to the Ma'mūnian map have been preserved. One example is a map of Egypt depicting the course of the Nile (Fig. 1.1, from a Ms. of al-Ḵwarizmī's Kitāb Ṣūrātu 'l-Arḏ[3]). This does not show any boundary between the Islamic lands of Muslim Upper and Lower Egypt, nor between Muslim Upper Egypt and the non-Islamic Nuba kingdom not far south of Asuan–a boundary well recognized not long after the conquest as shown by the so-called 'bakt,' a curious document, seemingly the only "peace treaty" concluded and honored for centuries

---

[1] State and territoriality concept–Lambton.

[2] al-Ḵwarizmī, Muhammad Ja'far Ibn Mūsā, *Das Kitāb Ṣūrātu 'l-Arḏ des Abu Jafār ibn Mūsā al-Ḵwarizmī*, ed. H. von Mzik (Leipzig, 1926).

[3] Map from Ms. of al-Ḵwarizmī's *Kitāb Ṣūrātu 'l-Arḏ*, Ms. COD 4247, Universitäts Bibliothek Strassburg as presented in Yusuf Kamal's *Monumenta Cartographica*, 1930, vol III, p. 524.

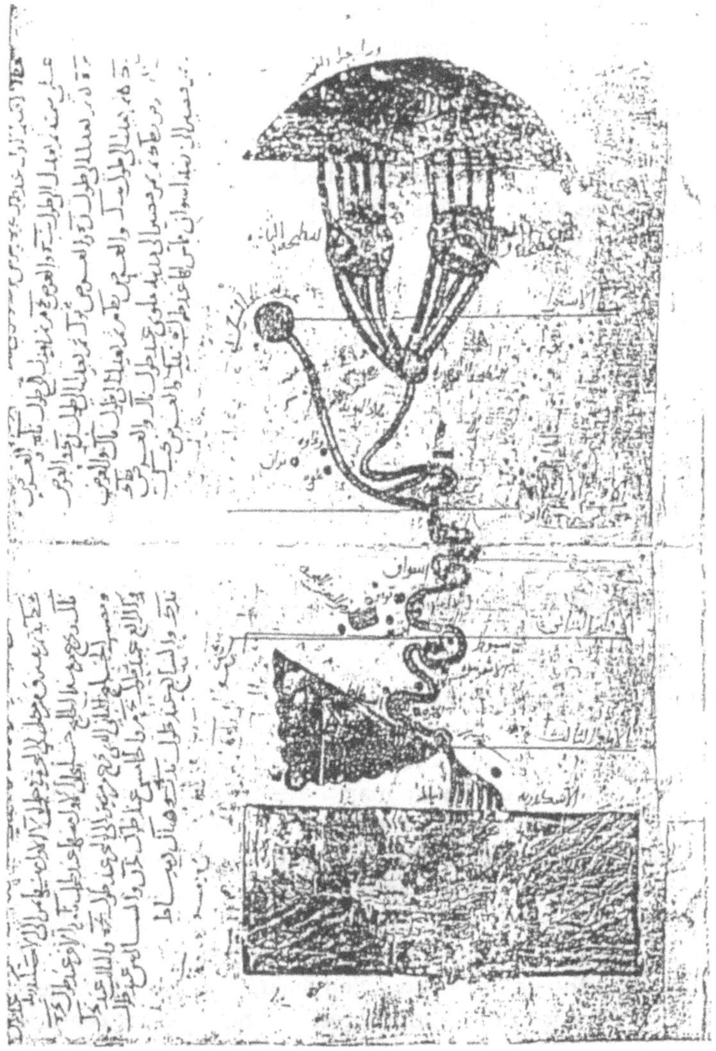

FIGURE 1.1. **Map of the course of the Nile of Egypt from a Ms. of al-K̲warizmī's *Kitāb Sūrātu 'l-Arḍ* dated 428 h = 1037 AD (the original of the book is dated before 218 h = 833AD). The straight lines running E–W represent the successive climates (*aqālīm*). Asuan is indicated just below the crease of the page, *belād nuba* is written in the triangular space between the Egyptian Nile and the Ethiopian Nile at the level marked *k̲att al-istiwā'*, the equator. No boundaries are shown—the line to the right of the Nile just above the level of Asuan is due to a crease as can be verified from other copies of this map.**

between Muslim and Infidel – in this case – Christian states.[4] These findings suggest – but are far from establishing conclusively – that, unlike Ptolemy's *Cosmographia*,[5] al-Ḵwarizmī's treatise did not include information on boundaries, and, by further inference, that this feature may also have been absent from the original Ma'mūnian map.

With later Arabo-Islamic maps one is on considerably firmer ground.[6] One can distinguish two major schools of Muslim cartography: the earlier Balkhi school that included the cartographers contributing to the various versions of the so-called Atlas Islamicus,[7] and the school of twelfth- and thirteenth-century geographers including al-Idrisi and those following his lead. A major representative of the Balkhi school is Ibn Ḥauqal whose maps form an integral part of his treatise on geography.[8] Out of a total of twenty-three maps included in his treatise, twelve showed no boundaries. The remaining eleven – including among others all of Ibn Ḥauqal's maps of the Middle East – did show boundaries labeled *ḥadd*, but what is shown under that designation is clearly devoid of geographical significance. In each case the detailed map sketches are encased in caligraphic and largely rectilinear frames designated as "*ḥ.................add al-fārs* or "*ḥ............add al-ḵuzistān*." Evidently, these (Fig. 1.2) cannot well bear any relation to real borderlines separating one of these states from another on the ground. This conclusion is made even more convincing by six of these maps showing in place of parts of the boundaries framing a given state *two* parallel caligraphic lines separated by a small distance, representing (and labeled as) the boundaries of two adjacent countries, for instance *al-fārs* and *al-ḵuzistān* (numbers 1 vs. 2 and 3, and 4a and b vs. 5, 6, and 7 in Figures 1.2a and b illustrate this for a rectangular and a circular 'frame'). Clearly, such double lines would have to coincide were they intended to represent a boundary *line* between two states.

Small scale circular world maps from the hand of several of the authors of this school have survived. These push the point further: they show whole regions subdivided into more or less rectangular boxes, each inscribed with the name of a country or a province (Fig. 1.3). The arrangement of these boxes relative to each other approaches randomness – assignment of a name to a given box bears little relation to the actual

---

4 The document circumvents the Qur'anic interdict against permanent peace with the infidel by posing as a commercial treaty.

5 Ptolemaeus, Claudius, *Cosmographia* (Rome 1478 ed.), Amsterdam, 1966. This work was transmitted to the Arabo-Islamic scholars at an early date; under khalif al-Ma'mūn it was translated into Arabic by a committee of scholars that seems to have included al-Ḵwarizmī. There is every indication that this work was germinal to the development of geographic science in the Islamic world. Boundaries are frequently referred to in the text accompanying the tables of geographic coordinates of the *Cosmographia*, typically in the form: A. comes to an end (*'terminat'*) at........, naming either a natural feature, like a river or a mountain range, or a line connecting well-defined places.

6 Cf. e.g., maps in Kamal, Yusuf, *Monumenta Cartographica Africae et Aegypti*, vols. III and IV (Leiden, 1932-1935).

7 Miller, K., *Mappae Arabicae (1926)*, ed. H. Glaube (Wiesbaden, 1986), 7-20.

8 Ibn ḥauqal, abu 'l-kasim, an-nasibī, *Kitāb ṣuratu 'l'arḍ*, ed. J.H. Kramers (Leiden, 1967).

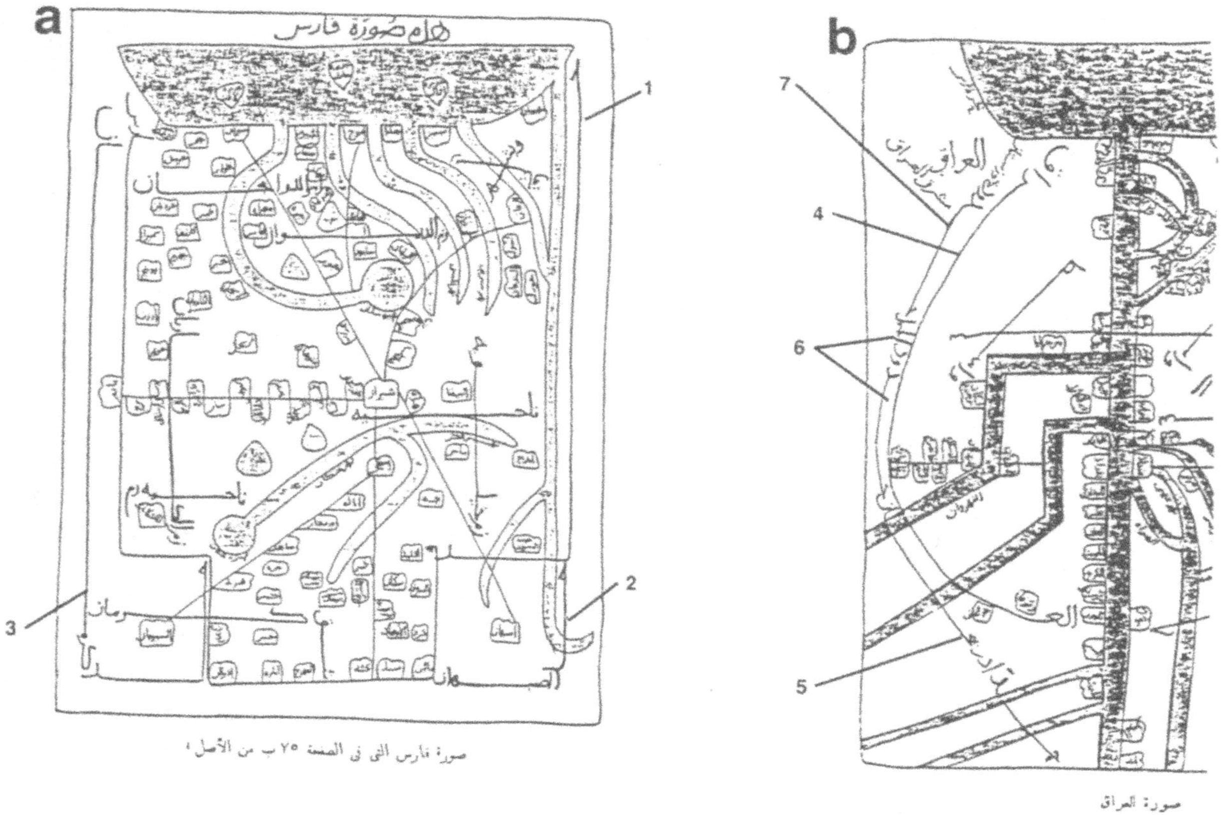

FIGURE 1.2. **Two maps from ibn Ḥauqal's *Kitāb ṣuratu 'l'arḏ* (Beyrouth 1992 edition), *a.. al-Fārs b. al-'irāq*. The text marked by the numbers reads: 1) *Ḥadd Fârs;* 2) *ḥadd isbahân;* 3) *ḥadd kirmân;* 4) *ḥadd al-'irâq;* 5) *ḥadd aḏrabijân;* 6) *hudûd al-jabal;* 7) *hudûd ḵûzistân.***

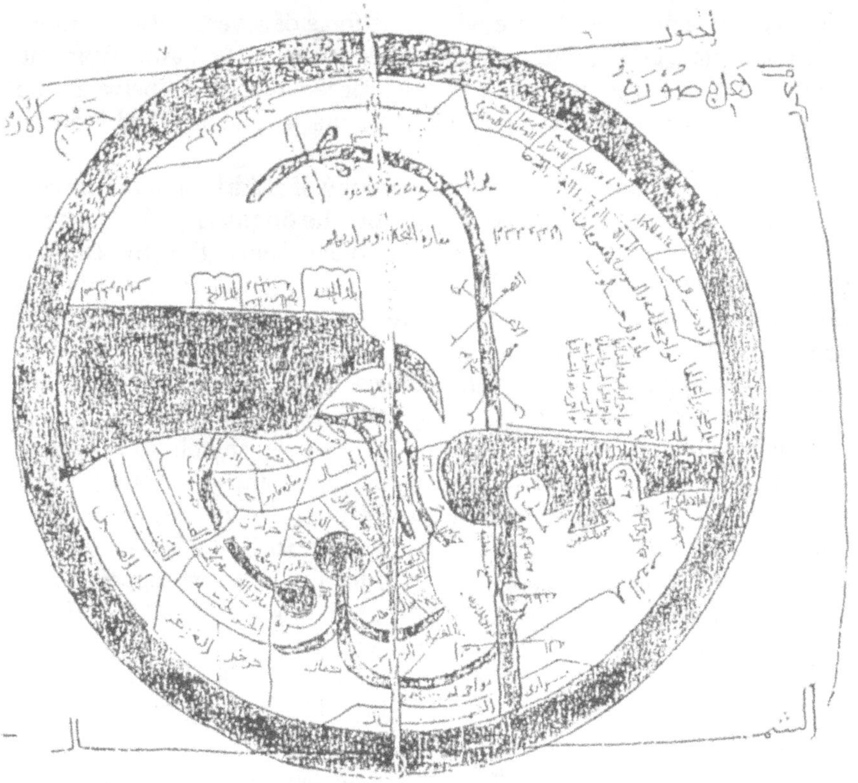

FIGURE 1.3. Example of a map of the entire inhabited world—*ṣūrat jamī' al-arḍ*—this one by Ibn Ḥauqal, 997 AD (the copy is from a Ms. dated 479 h i.e., 1086 AD) showing the arbitrary box-like indications of the confines of various realms, especially in Asia and the Near East in the lower left quadrant. As usual, the top of this map is South. The two large dark areas are the Indian Ocean on the left and the Mediterranean Sea on the right. The two smaller dark circles are the Caspian (Khazar) Sea and, probably, the Aral Sea. Constantinople and the Passage from the Mediterranean are indicated, but there is no recognizable trace of the Black Sea. The structure looking a bit like a shepherd's crook extending from the Eastern end of the Mediterranean toward the top and left is the Nile.

location of the state or province the name of which is enclosed by that box. Nor, indeed, does the size of the boxes bear any relation to the size of the country named.

Given these characteristics, I believe that it is not unjust to conclude that geographers of the period of the Balkhi school (i.e., the ninth and tenth centuries AD) recognized the existence of political boundaries in the sense that as one progressed in a direction away from the center of a state, one would sooner or later pass from one sovereignty to another or that one's taxes would flow to different places on either side of such a division. Yet, clearly in the minds of these cartographers such boundaries were constituted not as sharply defined boundary lines but rather as transition zones of uncertain sovereignty between two states. The image thus projected would seem to imply that these authors considered any given state as composed of a central core, the focus of its power and identity, and a peripheral zone where the force of sovereignty and identity of that state grew progressively feebler as one moved away from the capital, to be replaced gradually, as one proceeded on a line between the capitals of any two neighboring states, by the sovereignty and identity of the adjoining state.

This concept is born out by the cartography of al-Idrisi and his successors. I have had the opportunity to examine the originals of three manuscripts of al-Idrisi's great work[9]—the oldest one, the twelfth- or thirteenth-century Paris Ms. Bibl. Nat. F.A. #2221, and the later Bodleian Library's Mss. Pococke #345, and Greaves #42. In each case the inhabited world and the text describing it are conceived of as divided into 7 × 10 sections, corresponding to seven climates, *aqālim*, each further subdivided west to east into 10 sections, *ajzā'*;[10] each of the resulting 70 sections is provided with its own map.[11] I have been unable to trace any indication of boundaries in any of these maps, including specifically those representing regions where Ibn Ḥauqal's maps deployed their linear *ḥadd*, i.e., in the Middle East (sections III 5,6,7; IV 4,5,6; and V 4,5) and western Central Asia (IV and V 7,8) for the two first named Mss., and sections III 5,6,7 in the case of Greaves #42, as well as in all three Mss. in the sections representing Egypt as well as the North African coast between Egypt and the Atlantic (III 1–4). In place of boundaries one encounters expanded text such as "country of ʿIraq," or "country of the Nuba," written, e.g.,

"بلـــــــــــد نوبة"

which may be transcribed as

'bala__________d nûba'

placed across a region corresponding to the core of whatever entity is named, often surrounded by a more or less clear area separating it from neighboring units (Fig. 1.4). Thus, while al-Idrisi's maps do not include graphic indications of boundaries or boundary zones, they do mark out the core regions of the political units concerned. Only fragmentary evidence has come to light so far concerning Ibn Saʿid's cartography, but such as it is, it confirms the impression gained from comparison of the texts to the effect that he followed al-Idrisi in most respects, including omission of boundaries from his cartography.[12]

In sum, examination of maps by twenty-three Arabo-Islamic geographers[13] working between 820 and 1350 AD shows that boundaries are completely omitted from much of the cartography of the period, and

---

[9] al-Idrisī, al-šarīf, *Kitāb nuzha 'l muštāq fī-'ḵtirāq al-afāq- 'ālam al-kutub* (Beirut, 1989).

[10] The full text and accompanying maps are preserved in the case of Paris 2221 and Pococke 345, but only the first three climates, 30 sections in the case of Greaves 42.

[11] These seventy maps are more familiar in the form of a supposed world map, as they were assembled—mistakenly, I am convinced (cf. my "History of Muslim Geography," *Comparative Civilizations Review* 26 [1992] : 73–109), by Konrad Miller (*Mappae Arabicae* vol. 1, Stuttgart 1926).

[12] Ibn saʿid al-Magribī, *Kitāb basṭ al- arḏ fī 'ṭ -ṭ ūl wa-'l-ʿarḏ* (J.G. Ginés ed., Tetuan, 1958).

[13] A list of cartographers or map sources consulted is available.

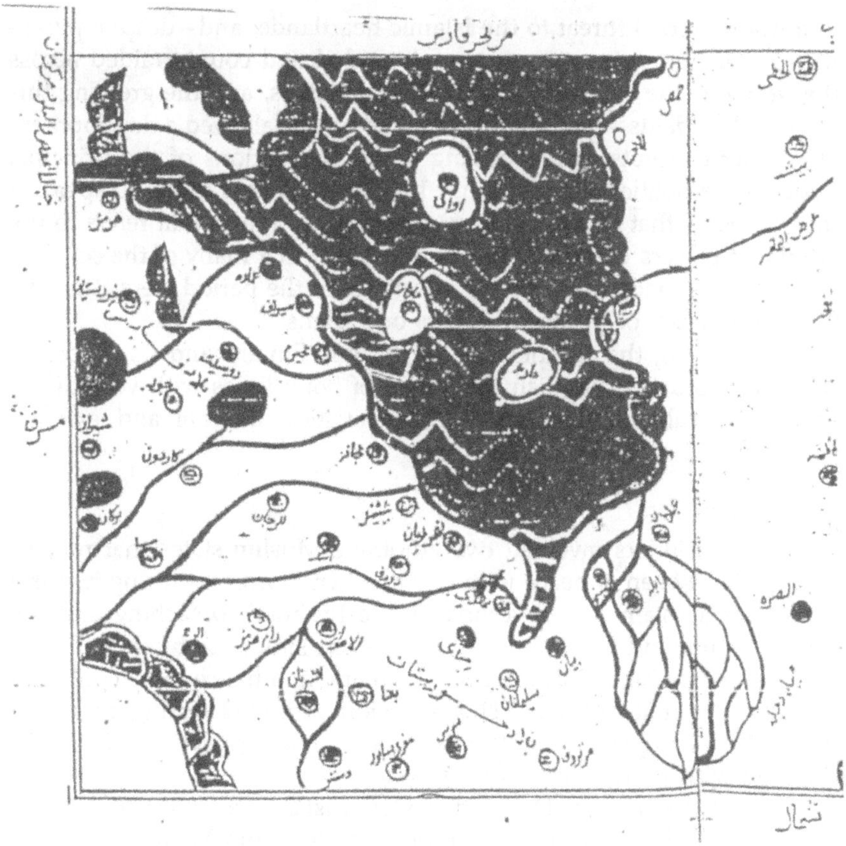

FIGURE 1.4. A sample of al-Idrisi's cartography, the sixth part of the second climate, representing the region around the northern end of the Persian Gulf (indicated by the dark area). As usual, the South is at the top. The delta of the Euphrates/Tigris is represented by the network of channels in the lower right quadrant. Note the complete absence of boundaries in spite of the fact that the map includes parts of Syria, Iraq, Khuzistan, and Fars. The characteristic expanded labeling of the inner lands or the central region of a recognized country is here illustrated by the labels *balād ḵu..........zistān* بلاد خ.....وزستان (bottom, center), and *balād f..........ārs* بلاد ف.......ارس (just above the horizontal middle, near the left margin).

are represented only by simple geometric lines having symbolic rather than geographic significance in the rest. The data suggest that each country was conceived of as being divided into a core including its center of power and a periphery separating that core from the nearest adjacent country.

Boundaries in the Arabo-Islamic Geographic and Historical Texts

Boundaries by their very nature are not neutral but are strongly conditioned by the political realities of the moment. It should be understood that the present survey of Arabo-Islamic documents bears essentially on the period of 440 years from about 750 to 1190 AD. This was relatively free from external threat to the Islamic heartlands, and—despite perennial minor fluctuations as opponents raided and counterraided across the frontiers, the emergence of internal divisions, and the growing turmoil in al-Andalus—can be considered as having allowed a development of frontier concepts corresponding to the inclinations of the principal actors in the politics of the realm.[14] It is permissible, I think, to speak of this period as that of Arabo-Islamic geography, a term that refers to the dominant players without attempting to deny that many of the scholars whose works made up the body of science of the period were Persians, Syrians, Greeks, or perhaps Berbers or Indians.

In discussing the frontiers of the Islāmic Empire and its successor states, one must distinguish two kinds of boundaries with very different ideological and geographic characteristics—internal and external boundaries.

Internal Frontiers

Internal frontiers involved two adjoining Muslim states that may or may not have been at peace with one another. However, during its early years, Dār al-Islām was governed by the Prophet's preaching and the Qurānic command that there all true believers should be brothers inhabiting one single 'umma under a single imām, and hence there could not exist any internal frontiers. This situation prevailed during the early stages of the conquest under the four first, "rightly guided" khalifs, and, although with some reservations, throughout the period of the reigns of the Umayyad khalifs of Damascus: Dār al-Islām was a single political unit under one ruler, at first the Prophet ruling from Medina, than the Prophet and subsequently the first khalifs ruling from Mecca, later on the Umayyad khalifs ruling from Damascus. This situation changed when the 'Abbasids of 'Iraq displaced the Umayyads in the second half of the eighth century. There followed almost immediately the beginning of the breakup of the Empire with the secession of al-Andalus under the rule of the Umayyads of Cordoba.

From the death of Muhammad, the khalifs responded to the increasing size of their dominions by delegating authority to umara' (pl. of amîr) who were in charge of the military campaigns as well as of religious affairs in the various provinces. Presently, when the first ebullience of the conquest had subsided somewhat and the matter of gathering revenues assumed greater prominence, 'umala' responsible for fiscal matters were associated with these religio-military officials. Given the widening spaces over which the Empire held sway and the limited means of communication available at the time, it should come as no surprise that these officers had to operate much of the time independently of the central government, and that with the passage of time they should assume considerable though variable degrees of autonomy. Under the Umayyads this tendency had been controlled in part by close personal relations between

[14] Vatikiotis, P.J., *Islam and the State* (London, 1987), 21.

the ruler and his delegates, and in part by assuring that the terms of office of many of the provincial governors were kept short.[15]

Under the 'Abbasids these constraints presently showed themselves insufficient, and one by one provincial governorships became increasingly autonomous and assumed hereditary character (cf, Fig. 1.5a[16]). Thus, the secession of al-Andalus was followed in less than 50 years in North Africa by that of the Idrisids of Marocco, and shortly afterwards by that of the Aghlabids of Ifriqiya and their successors the Fatimids, and a little later by those of the Tulunids and the Ikhshidids of Egypt. In northern Syria the Hamdanids ruled throughout most of the tenth century, while in the Iranian lands the Tahirids were effectively independent by 820 AD, to be succeeded by the 'Alids and the Saffârids within less than half a century. In the Khurasan and Transoxania the Samânids arose before the end of the ninth century and spread their rule into Persian regions. They in turn were succeeded by the Ghaznavids whose center of power eventually shifted southeast into Afghanistan and the Punjab.[17] All of these arose from provincial governors under khalifal suzerainty, and what had been formerly provinces of the khalifate presently became autonomous or *de facto* autonomous states with hereditary rulers, and with their own armies and revenues from which they devolved minimal or no part to the fisc at Baghdad. While some of the rulers still acknowledged the suzerainty of the Khalif of Baghdad at least formally, others chose to ignore him even as a matter of form, e.g., by no longer reading his name into the Ḵuṭba, the Friday prayer, or by deleting his name from their coins. By the eleventh century Seljuks, Seljuks of Rum, Fatimids, Khwarezmshahs, Almoravids, and Ghaznavids between them had assumed the rule of virtually all of the Islāmic territories, leaving the kalifate with little more than the city of Baghdad—and that only under the watchful tolerance of Buwaihid or Seljuk masters.

The pattern emerging is graphically represented in Figure 1.5b: where Muhammad had envisioned a single unified realm dominated by a single theocratic ruler, the ḵalifa, within 150 years after his death we find two units. Thereafter the number of successor states continued to increase rapidly and progressively over the next 300 years so that by the time the Mongols extinguished the remnants of the kalifate in the mid thirteenth century the realm of Islām had been split up into fifteen separate Muslim-ruled states. The history of these successor states includes numerous instances of warfare between some of these entities. Thus, the breakup of the Islāmic Empire was associated with the formation of numerous successor states that in turn entailed the establishment between them of numerous "internal boundaries."

---

[15] Short terms of amirs under Umayyads.

[16] Lane-Poole, S., *The Mohammedan Dynasties* (New Delhi, 1986) after pp. XVI and XX.

[17] Cf. e.g., Bishai, W.B., *Islamic History of the Middle East* (Boston, 1968). Part IX, *Regional Dynasties during the Late 'Abbasid Period.*

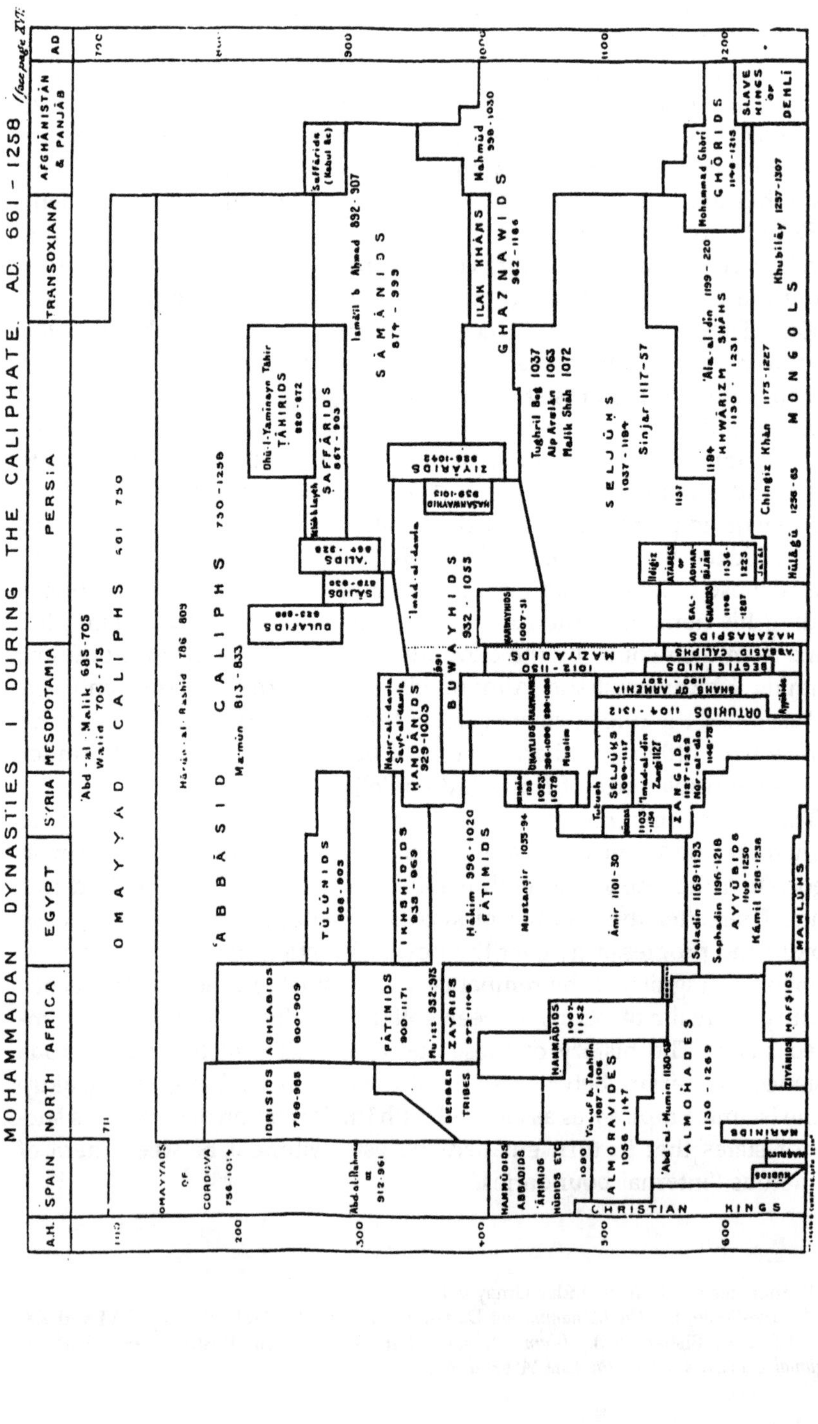

FIGURE 1.5a. Proliferation of dynasties and states in the Islāmic Empire from its inception to the time of the extinction of the khalifate (from: Lane-Poole, s., *The Mohammedan Dynasties*, New Delhi, 1893).

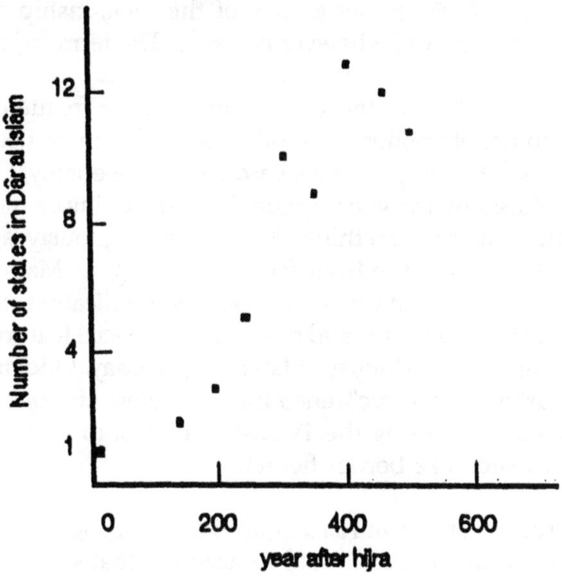

FIGURE 1.5b. Number of coexisting dynasties in the realm of the Islāmic Empire as a function of time over the same period as 1.5a.

External Frontiers

External frontiers occurred at the periphery of the empire wherever a Muslim polity adjoined an 'Unbeliever' one. They were recognized from early on as frontiers facing *dār al-ḥarb*, the land of war of the Qurānically mandated permanent state of Holy War. In the period here under consideration this had come to be interpreted as implying that they were inevitably and permanently frontiers of war even when at a given moment armies were not marching upon one another.

Terminology

Before proceeding further with the discussion of the actual configuration of these two types of boundaries, it is necessary to pause for a moment to consider the terminology used in the literature to refer to the geographic concepts representing the transition from one polity to another.

Of the Arabic terms denoting some kind of boundary (cf. footnote)[18]

---

[18] The Arabo-Islamic authors made use of a number of Arabic terms to designate a concept sometimes properly translatable as 'boundary':

1. *ākīr* = آخير ...... the extreme part of anything, including provinces or countries or many kinds of geographically definable pieces of land or sea;
2. *takūm* = تخوم ...... from *takama* = to fix the limits of anything; the noun is translated as boundary, limit, border; *mutâkhim* = متاخم is used to mean adjacent or neighboring.
3. *ḥāšīa* = حاشية .... margin (of book), border, seam, edge.
4. *farj* = فرج .... related to *farjah* meaning a mountain or other pass, and occasionally translatable as border (as e.g., between Sind and Multân, i.e., muslim and kafr).

three (*āk̲īr, tak̲ūm, ḥāšīa*) imply a view of the relationship strictly from within–the end or limit of whatever is inside. The term *farj* implies two-way flow of traffic like that across a mountain pass.

In practice, only three of these ten terms were in frequent use by the geographers to denote political boundaries: *Ḥadd* can be taken to imply a hostile relation–the edge of the sword facing the enemy. On the other hand, as employed by the geographers it seems to imply most often no more than the end of something. More unambiguously aggressive is *t̲ugūr* (original meaning: the front fangs of a dog!); its Mamluk replacement is *nīb*. Finally, *'awāṣim* carries a defensive implication, the holding-off of an enemy from without, and designates a special feature of external boundary systems, to be discussed later in this essay. One may mention finally the Turkish term "uç" encountered below in connection with events in Asia Minor during the Turkish conquest to designate 'border' in compound words like border fighter.

Ḥadd *versus* t̲ugūr. The term *Ḥadd* is used by the geographers wherever it is intended that the reader should understand that some geographical entity came to an end. Thus we find it applied not only to countries, but also to cities, to the domain of Islâm, to land as opposed to the sea, to the end of a mountain range, or to the great desert and others.

In its political sense *Ḥadd* was used frequently by Ibn Ḥauqal (cf. Fig. 1.2), by al-Istakhri,[19] but also by al-Idrisi[20] in the description of the confines of specific regions within the realm of the Islamic Empire: Egypt, some of the countries of the Middle East, the Sind–but hardly anywhere else. One may encounter further specification, by description of the general configuration of the implied boundary both in terms of the countries or peoples on the other side of various portions of the

---

5. *ḥadd* = حد ...... primary meaning: cutting edge of knife of sword; then: edge, boundary, border, limit, terminus (also, in other contexts, punishment for acts forbidden by the Qur'an).
6. *t̲agr* = ثغر ..... primary meaning: front teeth (as shown by an angry dog–though Lane emphasizes what appears to be the opposite concept, the hinder end of a mount or a beast of burden, the place whence one drives it forwards); port (of departure), harbor, as well as (military) frontier town, or frontier district facing an enemy; the plural, *t̲ugūr* = ثغور designates a frontier zone or march, and sometimes a boundary.
7. *nīb, pl. anīāb* = نيب ... lit. canine tooth, fang; used in Mamluk times for frontier defenses in place of *t̲ugūr*, a term that by that time had gone out of general usage.
8. *'asim* = عصم .... from 'aṣama–to hold back, hinder. The noun is used to designate towns less exposed than the *t̲ugūr* but yet lying near enough enemy territory to be of military significance. The plural, 'awāṣim = عواصم designates a zone defined by the presence of a number of 'awāṣim and lying behind the zone of t̲ugūr.

Finally one may mention the Persian terms *marz* = مرز .... a limit, border, boundary of a country or a field and not used in Arabic texts, but probably the origin of the term 'marca' in Romance languages or march in English and Mark in German and related languages.

[19] al-Iṣṭak̲rī, abu isḥaq al-fārisī, *Kitāb masālik al-mamālik* (de Goeje, M.J. ed.), 3rd ed. (Leiden, 1967).

[20] al-Idrisī, al-šarīf, *Kitāb nuzha 'l muštāq fī-k̲tirāq al-afāq* (Beirut, 1989).

boundary, and, albeit merely in very general terms—by reference to the direction in which boundary portions lie with respect to the central country that they delimit: "On the East, the *ḥadd* of Egypt faces the Sea of Qulzum, then it bends to face the Kingdom of the Baja, then runs between the Land of the Nuba and Egypt. . . ." Mountain ranges, occasionally a town, and rivers may be named as defining such a frontier, although more commonly rivers and the valleys they create are occupied by a single political unit. As in the case of the Sea of Qulzum (the Red Sea), sea shores provide sharply defined boundaries, and indeed this is implied by border formalities in ports to be discussed in a subsequent section. In some cases one finds the transition from one country to another denoted merely by reference to a town: "The first town in the west of Ifriqiya is, . . ." presumably implying progress on a road of some kind, usually not further defined. All parts not defined in these simple terms are left vague.[21] The concept of *hudūd* as described in this manner is well represented by the decorative lines or arcs encountered in Ibn Ḥauqal's maps (Fig. 1.2): generalized designations, indicating that two political units abut on each other in a given region, but without any intention of providing a precise definition of an actual *line* of separation—a frontier zone enveloping a central core in the same sense as the cartographers' symbols, rather than a boundary line of demarcation defining a realm within which the power of the central government is felt uniformly. This concept also corresponds to the pattern of labeling used throughout by al-Idrisi as described above (cf. Fig. 1.4). The only exceptions to this perception are in relation to sea coasts and seaports, and to the few places where the boundary follows the course of a river: here the natural feature defines the boundary sharply.

All told, therefore, both texts and cartographic representation thus concur in implying a concept of boundaries *within* the broad confines of the Islamic Empire that is not that of a sharp transition from one political entity to the next, but rather a gradual interpenetration of the adjoining communities, reflecting a political reality well described by Hourani: "Before the modern age frontiers were not clearly or precisely delimited . . . one should rather think of the power of a dynasty as radiating from a number of urban centers with a force that tended to grow weaker with distance. . . ."[22]

Elsewhere I have suggested that Muslim geography of the Middle Ages is a linear geography, conceived in terms of a network of lines of communication between cities.[23] One might expect that in such a representation *ḥudūd* might intersect these lines of communication to define points where one passed from one sovereignty to the next, marked per-

---

[21] Cf. e.g., al-ʿumarī, ibn faḏl allah, *Masālik al-abṣār fī al-mamālik al-amsār*, Gaudefroy-Demombynes trans. (Paris, 1927), 99.

[22] Hourani, A., *A History of the Arab Peoples* (Cambridge, 1991), 145.

[23] Brauer, R.W., "Geography in the Muslim World," *Compar. Civiliz. Rev.* 27 (1992): 73–110.

haps by a customs station; as will be shown in Section 2 this is not the case, and travelers' reports corroborate the sense of absence of sharp boundaries we gleaned from the cartographers.

The second term, *t̲agr*, while at times translated as boundary, in fact represents a more complex reality. The original sense mentioned above has persisted in modern Arabic where it still designates a port or a harbor. Alexandria was often referred to in the Geniza documents as '*the t̲agr*,'[24] the ports of the Levant further to the north also were known collectively as 'the *t̲ugūr* (*al-baḥrīa*)'–in both cases reflecting the aversion of the early Muslim rulers to what they perceived as a sea dominated by hostile forces.[25]

This idea presently was applied not only to ports on the seashore but extended to places on land. In both the Near East and al-Andalus the earliest usage of the term *t̲agr* referred to the region just in front of the armies facing the Christian enemy. Presently, the singular came to be used primarily to designate specific localities in a more stable frontier zone, fortified places that served as residence and staging points for warriors engaged in carrying the *jiḥād*–the Holy War–to adjacent enemy lands beyond the confines of *Dār al-Islām*. Such places might shelter *ribāṭ*, the quasi-monastic fortified establishments housing those fully dedicated to fulfilling this religious obligation (as e.g., in Ibn Ḥauqal's *Kitāb ṣuratu 'l'arḏ* where, among a number of places, he mentions that the people of Damascus established a *ribāṭ* in the neighboring *t̲agr* of *Antartus*). The regions in which such fortified places were located necessarily lay in the frontier zone between Muslim and enemy (unbeliever) countries, and in the literature of the times came to be referred to as the *t̲ugūr.* Indeed, the term was used exclusively for frontiers of this kind. Table 1.1 shows that, while boundaries were recognized between Arabo-Islamic, Iranian and Turkish polities and lands dominated by many ethnic groups, *t̲ugūr* were recorded when and only when the adjoining territory was dominated by non-Islamized peoples.[26]

---

24 Lapidus, I.M, ed. *Middle Eastern Cities* (Berkeley CA, 1969), 82.

25 Hourani, G.F., *Arab Seafaring* (New York, 1975), 53-54.

26 One may test the importance of the ethnic as opposed to the religious factor in relation to boundary formation in the Islāmic Empire by asking whether ethnic differences influenced the formation of the militarized kind of boundary zone designated as t̲ugūr in the course of such armed conflict. Table 1.1 lists contacts between the several comprehensive categories of ethnic encountered in the course of the history of the Islāmic Empire over the first eight centuries following the revelation to the Prophet, and relates these to the presence between such pairs of states of recognizable political borders as well as of t̲ugūr, the militarized kind of border zone.

The categories established in this fashion allow one to distinguish three non-vacant classes: 'neither type of boundary observed'; 'political boundaries but no thughûr'; and 'political boundaries with thughûr' (a fourth category, 'thughûr without political boundary' is physically impossible). The twelve groups of pairs of neighbors identified in this fashion are distributed between these three classes so that two fall into the first one, four into the second, and six into the last. When the several polities are further separated into those professing Islâm, either from its inception or as recent converts–and those that do not do so–(Christian and Hindu) (Table 4.4) it is found that in the six cases involving two adjoining Muslim states there were no t̲ugūr, even where the states had been engaged in armed

Table 1.1. Ethnic Factors in Boundary Structure in the Medieval Muslim World

Conquerors	Residents	Ṯuġūr	Political frontier
Arabs	Yemenites	0	0
"	Iraqis	0	0
"	Iranians	0	+
"	c. A. Turks	+	+
"	Hindus	+	+
"	Rum	+	+
"	Armenians	+	+
"	Egyptians	0	+
"	Berbers	0	+
"	Franks and Visigoths	+	+
Turks	Rum	+	+
"	Armenians	+	+
"	Iranians	0	+

Muslims vs.	No political borders	Borders, no Ṯuġūr	Ṯuġūr
Early Converts	2	4	0
Christians	0	0	4
Polytheists	0	0	2

Ṯuġūr as thus interpreted represented a no-man's land studded with smaller fortresses that served as the first line of defense for the adjacent regions of Muslim states as well as staging points and places of refuge for raids into kāfir territory. Examples of such usage are *ṯuġūr aš-šāmiah* in the north of Syria, *ṯuġūr al-jazirīa* between Mesopotamia and Armenia and Anatolia, forming part of the *ṯuġūr aš-šāmiah, ṯuġūr at-turuk* (those "mā warā' 'n-nahr," i.e., in Transoxania beyond the river Oxus, at the eastern margin of Khorasan facing the still heathen Turks), or in al-Andalus *ṯuġūr al-adnā', –al-awṣat*, and *–al-a'lā* (those between the western, the central, and the eastern parts, respectively, of Al-Andalus and the adjoining portions of Castilla, Leon/Aragon, and Provence). Between the

struggle, while in all six cases where Muslim and non-Muslim states abutted border zones were described that were functionally and structurally indistinguishable from the ṯuġūr between northern Syria or Mesopotamia and the lands of the Byzantine Empire. Persistence of these structures, furthermore, was not restricted to cases where the Muslim forces were the conquerors at the time; in al-Andalus, in northern Syria and al-Jazira, as well as in Anatolia, ṯuġūr or analogous zones persisted even where the Muslim forces had been compelled to retreat. In all these cases, however, the original development of a march had been associated with an advance of Muslim forces into enemy territory.

These results suggest that boundary zones of Muslim states assumed the character of ṯuġūr when, and only when, boundaries were formed between a Muslim and a non-Muslim state and hence were associated with a permanent state of Holy War; the phenomenon thus seems unrelated to ethnic differences between neighboring states, and unrelated, too, to the nature of the ethnic cleavages in the participating societies. The kind of evidence available does not allow one to decide whether the determining factor was that there was a religious difference between the two sides, or whether the result deduced from Table 4.4 is a consequence of the fact that wherever there was a state of Holy War, warfare necessarily was protracted and repetitive. The data thus are compatible with but not probative of the paramount significance of the religious factor as such in shaping the structure of boundaries involving Muslim societies on one or on both sides.

zone of the *ṯuġūr* and the interior Muslim realm an additional military zone known as *ʿawāṣim* was interposed in some places, notably on the Cilicio-Armenian frontier (Fig. 1.6) and in parts of the Andalusian *ṯuġūr.*

The perception of the *ṯuġūr* as denoting a zone, rather than merely the series of points suggested by the writings of the geographers, reflects in part the original usage referring to the frontier between Muslim and Christian as 'the *ṯaġr*'; in part, too, it most probably reflected Near Eastern political thinking that was strongly city-oriented and tended to view the combination of an urbanized place and the surrounding rural areas as pertaining to a single common unit – a district – several of which might make up the next higher political or administrative entity, known in al-Andalus as the *'kura'*.[27] The border districts were distinguished from *kuras* in the central portions of Syria/Mesopotamia or of al-Andalus by being given special administrative, and often taxation regimes, distinct from the core parts of the Islāmic Empire. In particular, they were under the control of a military commander, *qaʿīd,* and their link to the center tended to be much more tenuous than that for regular kuras in the consolidated parts of the state. Indeed, the holders of these appointments fulfilled many of the functions of a regular ruler and at times might act in defiance of the wishes of the central government. It is hardly surprising that there was a tendency for these posts to become hereditary, leading to the foundation of dynasties. In the nature of things, these in turn were apt to become foci for rebellion.[28]

The military importance of the *ṯuġūr* in the Middle East as well as in al-Andalus decreased rapidly after the middle of the eleventh century, but even after it had all but vanished these places retained a not insignificant role as centers for the exchange of merchandize between Muslim and Christian lands.

Examples from Near East and in al-Andalus. Ṯuġūr were described in all regions where Muslim territory abutted upon non-Muslim lands: In al-Andalus, in southern Egypt, in Syria, in Mesopotamia, in the Khurasan, and in the Makran. The significance of the usages of the terms described in the preceding paragraphs can be illustrated by the history of the con-

---

[27] Cf. the extensive discussion of the administrative and geographical terminology relative to these entities in: Bosch Vilá, J., "Consideraciones sobre al-ṯaġr en el Andalus y la division politico-administrativa de la España musulmana," in: *Études d'Orientalisme dediées à la mémoire de Lévi-Provençal,* vol. 1. (Paris, 1962), 20–33. Note specifically remission of the jizīa for the border population of the Jarâjima (EI 2, p. 456) and Glick, T.F., *Islamic and Christian Spain in the Early Middle Ages* (Princeton Univ. Press, 1979), 104 and 105 reorganization of frontier zones under the Umayyads.

[28] Examples are the Bani Qasi in the Upper March and their near independence of Cordoba (Glick, cf. above), 103, and Lévi-Provençal, vol. IV-1 (cf. above), 101–104, who concludes ". . . always unstable and the authority of Cordoba was never fully accepted for any length of time" and mentions, besides the Banu Qasi, Bahlul Marzuq, and Ibn Chilliqi, and a revolt in Merida that was not fully suppressed until 930 AD; Chejne, A.J. in : *Muslim Spain: its History and Culture* (U. of Minnesota Press, 1974), 50 ff. lists revolts of Dhu 'l-Nûn of Toledo in 1016–1085, al-Aflâs of Badajoz, Banu Hûd of Zaragoza in 1040–1042 AD.

FIGURE 1.6. Map of the area of contact between Byzantium (византия), Armenia (Арминия), and Northern Syria/Mesopotamia (Джазира) in the first half of the ninth century. The Black Sea is in the left upper corner labeled Понт, a small corner of the Mediterranean Sea shows in the lower left hand corner, labeled Средиземное Море. In the lower right corner are the two border regions between Byzantium and the Khalifal territories: сугур = *tuġūr*, and авасим = ʿawāṣim. From: *Aprenur u Apadckuú* by A.H. Tep, Zeboregíix Epebase, 1977, p. 169

cept in the two regions where it would seem to have played the greatest role – in the near East and in al-Andalus.

In the Near East the dynamics of the conquest established a frontier facing the Byzantine Empire well before the end of the seventh century, and, despite wavering of the line with successive raids and counterraids, this frontier zone shifted remarkably little for several centuries, until near the end of the Buyid domination of the Khalifate in the thirteenth century and the beginning collapse of Byzantine rule in Anatolia before the Turkish onslaught.[29] A defensive and staging zone was recognized as early as the reign of 'Umar ibn 'Abd al-Ḵattab and referred to as *ṯagr.* While widespread flight of the local population resulted in extensive depopulation of the zone, deliberately enhanced by forced depopulation under such Byzantine emperors as Heraclius,[30] some of the towns of an earlier date survived and a number of fortified new ones were established to serve as centers housing warriors as well as to as to serve – especially at a later date – as centers for cross-border exchange of merchandize. It is these towns that came to be referred to by the geographers as the *ṯuġūr* and that gave their collective name to the zone. In the spaces between these cities numerous lesser fortified sites seem to have existed,[31] strengthening the character of the zone to provide defense in some depth (cf. Table 1.2 below). The near eastern *ṯuġūr* were subdivided at the latest under the Khalif Harûn ar-Rashîd into Syrian and the Jazirían *ṯuġūr* (*ṯuġūr ash-shâmiya* and *ṯuġūr al-jazirīa*) with capitals in Tarsus and in Malatiya respectively. The distribution of these *ṯuġūr* in the works of the geographers suggests a defensive line of cities as illustrated in Figure 1.7 and 1.10. The designation seems to have persisted for some time after shifts in the military front had abolished the military significance of these *ṯuġūr.* As mentioned above, during the early centuries of Islamic domination this zone was backed by a second zone of primarily defensive significance, the *'awāṣim.* This is illustrated for the case of the North Syrian frontier with the capital of this particular 'âsima in Antiochia (cf. Fig. 1-6 for a modern reconstruction of the map of the region; sugur and avasim are the Russian transcripions of *ṯuġūr* and *'awāṣim*).[32] With the passage of time the distinction seems to have become blurred (thus already both Ibn Ḵordaḏba and Qudâma speak of both under the single term *awâsim* when reporting the revenues of 400,000 or 360,000 dinar from the region), and by the twelfth century the entire frontier zone came to be referred to as the *ṯuġūr.* The difference between the inner portions of the Islāmic Empire and this insecure frontier zone is well illustrated in the descriptions of Ibn Jubair, the returning pilgrim, who calls attention to the fact that as one came close to the northern limits of the Jebel Lubnān (on

---

[29] Honigmann, E., *Die Ostgrenze des Byzantinischen Reiches von 363 bis 1071* (Bruxelles, 1935).

[30] Canard, M., in EI-1, vol. 8, article: *'awāṣim* p. 761.

[31] Honigmann, E., EI-1, article: thughūr, vol. 8, p. 739, and M. Canard article: *'awāṣim* in: EI-2, vol. 1, p. 761; and Table 2 below.

[32] Ter-Jervondian, *Armenia i Arabskii Khalifat* (Erevan, 1977), 151–154.

Table 1.2. Towns[b] Designated as *ṯugūr* in Writings of Medieval Arabo-Islamic Geographers

no. of author	1	2	3	4	5	6	7	8	9	10	11	12	13	14	15	16	17	18
year AD	850	851	902	903	908	982	988	997	1000	1150	1154	1225	1228	1250	1286	1300	1368	1375
towns																		
Asuan						\\\\												
Tarsus				\\\\			\\\\					\\\\	\\\\	\\\\		\\\\		\\\\
Antakia															\\\\			
al-Iskanderia													\\\\		\\\\			
Malatia	\\\\				\\\\		\\\\											
al-Masisa			\\\\	\\\\			\\\\											
Mar`ash	\\\\				\\\\		\\\\											
Antartus					\\\\													
Adhana							\\\\									\\\\		
Washjird		\\\\														\\\\		
al-Harunia							\\\\									\\\\		
Farbar		\\\\																
Samat			\\\\															
Sariq			\\\\															
Isfijab							\\\\								\\\\			
Fil			\\\\															
Bira													\\\\		\\\\			
Bughras															\\\\			
Ra's al-Kana'is																\\\\		
Dailam										\\\\			\\\\					
al-Kanisa					\\\\		\\\\											
Qazuin	\\\\								\\\\									
Totila																	\\\\	
Wadi 'l-hajara							\\\\		\\\\									
Tarsuna																	\\\\	
Zamorra																	\\\\	
Santarin																	\\\\	
Sarqasta															\\\\		\\\\	
Larida															\\\\			
Barbuna															\\\\			
Tolitia							\\\\									\\\\		
`ain zurba							\\\\											
Tartusha							\\\\											
Saragossa																	\\\\	
Med. as-Salam																	\\\\	
Marida							\\\\											
Nafza							\\\\											
Ṯ. al a`āla															\\\\	\\\\		
Ṯ. al-awsāt															\\\\	\\\\		
Ṯ. al-adnā															\\\\	\\\\		
Ṯ. at-turuk	\\\\				\\\\													
Ṯ. al-jazīra	\\\\				\\\\		\\\\				\\\\							
Ṯ. al-bahr	\\\\																	
Ṯ. an-nūba	\\\\							\\\\										
Ṯ. aš-šām	\\\\				\\\\		\\\\											

nos./ names of authors:

1. Ibn Khordadhb
2. ibn ya'qubi
3. ibn al faqih
4. ibn rostah
5. al-istakhri
6. hudud al-`alam
7. ibn hauqal
8. al-muqaddasi
9. al-andalusi
10. az-zuhri
11. al-idrisi
12. ad-dimashqi
13. yaqut
14. al-qazuini
15. ibn sa`id
16. abu 'l-feda
17. al-himyari
18. ibn khaldun

[b] in Syria, al-Jazīra, Khurasān, al-Andalus, Egypt

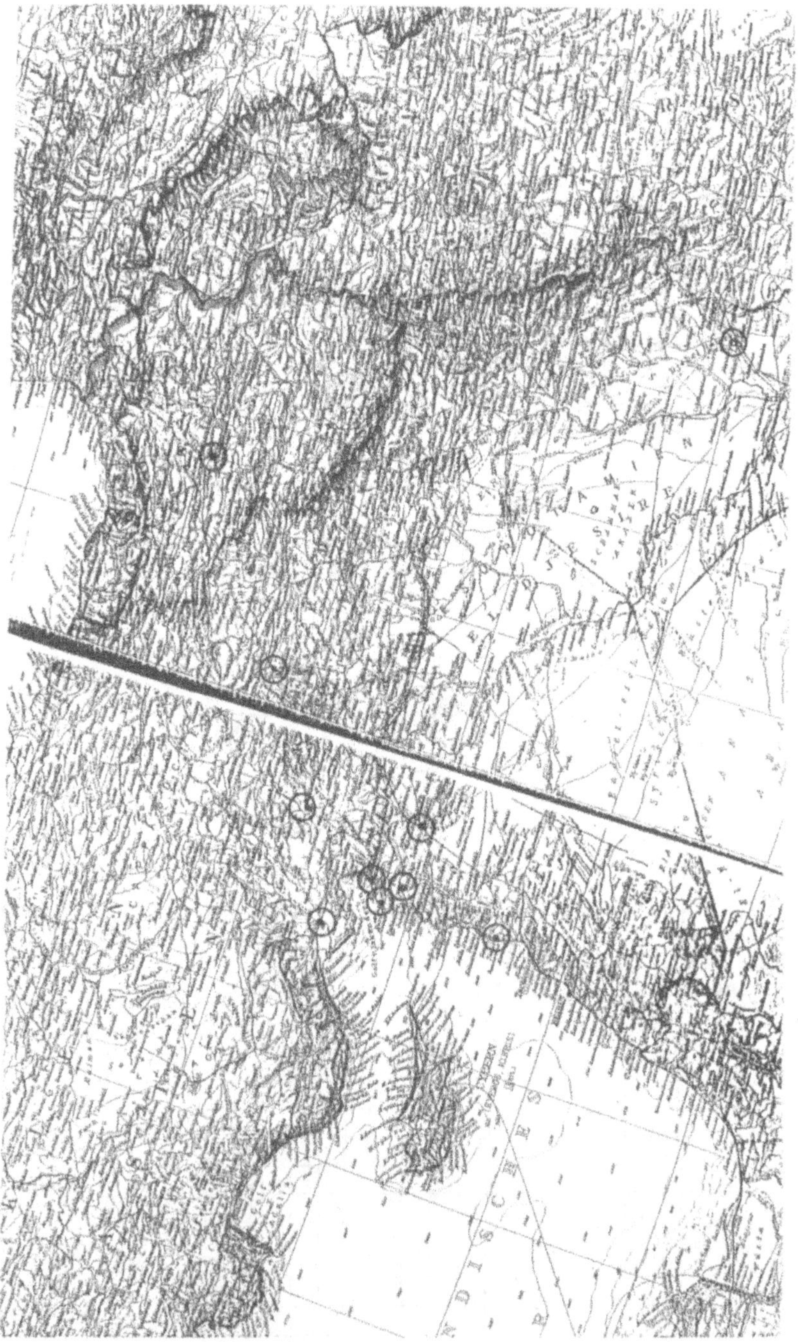

FIGURE 1.7. Modern map of the same general area as shown in Figure 1.6 with towns identified in the writings of the Arabo-Islamic geographers as *ṯuğūr* marked by black circles.

the other side of which the first Crusader towns were then located) the ḵāns, that is, the travelers' inns, became veritable fortresses with strong iron gates.[33]

The population of the countryside of these boundary zones, and especially of the fortified towns therein, was mixed. It included some of the original population, mainly Syrians and Armenians, Arabs—mainly, it seems, Qaisites—from the invading troops, as well as Zott, a wandering people, perhaps ancestors of the later gypsies and originating in India,[34] irregular border warriors, and the *jarājīma*, somewhat lukewarm Christians who served the Arabs as spies and scouts, especially after the capture of Antioch, in return for cash emoluments as well as remission of the *jizīa*, the head tax normally imposed upon non-Muslims residing in Muslim territory.[35]

In the case of *al-Andalus*, a zone of contact between the invading Muslims and the defending Christians was established early, and well before the turn of the seventh century was referred to at times as *the ṯagr* of al-Andalus, presumably reflecting the original metaphoric concept of the threatening teeth presented by an angry dog to his opponent.[36] In short order this came to be a sort of no-man's land, avoided by Christian inhabitants to whom this region, abutting on the Marca Hispanica, the Spanish Marches, had become 'terrae desertae.' The zone was presently provided with a network of fortresses, including sites like Saragossa, left over from an earlier time, as well as newly established strong points like *medīnat as-salām*, i.e., Medinaceli, and came to be referred to by the collective "the ṯugūr" (Fig. 1.8). In the course of the next decades the Muslim-controlled portion of the Iberian Peninsula became more or less stabilized, and for some time thereafter Muslim authors conceived of the Peninsula as divided by a largely imaginary range of mountains, the šarrāt or Sierra (or could it have been 'the Badlands' from the Arabic root *ash-šarrun*?) running west-east from the Mediterranean two-thirds of the way to the Atlantic at about the latitude of Toledo;[37] even in the twelfth century, in the sectional maps of al-Idrisi's Book of Roger, significant parts of this imaginary range are preserved to separate *'arḍ castilīa'* from *'arḍ al—andalus'* (Fig. 1.9).

Shortly after the arrival and accession of the Umayyads to the western Amirate, around 753 AD, this border zone was partitioned into Upper and Middle *ṯugūr*. In the course of the following decades it was further divided into subzones, the Upper, Middle and Lower (*al-adnā, al-awṣaṭ, al-aʿlā*) *ṯugūr* (Fig. 1.8a), a partition between Muslim and Christian lands

---

[33] Ibn Jubaīr (*1144-1218 AD*)- *Riḥla* (Dar Beyrut, 1974), 229.

[34] Ferrand, G., article "Zott" in EI-1, vol. VIII, p. 1235.

[35] Canard, M., in: EI-II, vol. 3, article Djaradjima, 436–438.

[36] Bosch Vilá, J., "Consideraciones sobre el *ṯagr* en el Andalus y la division politico administrativa de la España Musulmana" in: *Études d'Orientalisme dediées à la mémoire de Lévi-Provençal*, vol. 1 (Paris 1962), pp. 23-33.

[37] Giménez, F.H., "El convencional espinazo montañoso de orientación este-oeste que los geógrafos arabes attribuyen a la Peninsula Ibérica," al-Andalus 30 (1965): 201–275.

FIGURE 1.8a. The Iberian Peninsula showing the approximate configuration of the *ṯugūr* in the tenth century (from: Fletcher, R., *Moorish Spain*, New York, NY, 1992, p. 51).

that seems to have been recognized almost to the very end in the late twelfth century when Muslim holdings in the Iberian Peninsula had become restricted to the region south of Cordoba.[38] Figure 1-8b illustrates that the detailed configuration of the *ṯugūr* could be very complex, representing the results of successive local engagements. As in the Middle East, a more vaguely recognized zone south of the ṯugūr was called the *'awāṣim*, towns assigned a defensive role, but the distinction between *ṯugūr* and *'awāṣim* became increasingly vague as time went on.[39]

The population of the *ṯugūr* in al-Andalus as in the Near East differed in some respects from that of the more central kuras. In particular during

[38] Lévi-Provençal, E., *España Musulmana*, vols. V of Historia de España, R.M. Pidál ed., Madrid, 1957, p. 32 ff. and cf. 'lamina V' in Bosch Vilá.

[39] Cf. Ibn Ḥauqal for fine examples of the waxing and waning of the fortunes of such boundary places as malatia; also cf. ref. 25 above.

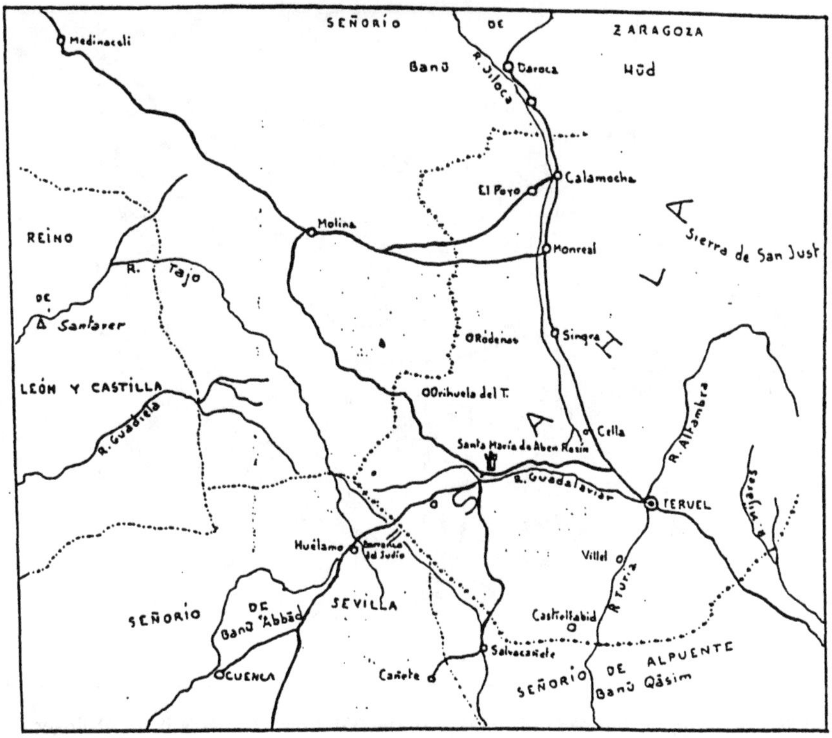

FIGURE 1.8b. Map of a region in the Middle March of al-Andalus at 1086 AD illustrating the interdigitation of nominal districts at the frontier between Leon and Castile and the Muslim dominions (from: Bosch Vilá, J., *Albarracin Musulman*, Vol. I, Teruel, 1959, p. 63).

the early centuries after the conquest they provided homesteads for members of the conquering armies. In the middle and lower *ṯuġūr* these were made up in large part of Berbers–derived from sedentary rather than nomad tribes prior to the incursion of the Almohads–while in the upper (i.e., the most easterly) *ṯuġūr* the Arabs formed the dominant element.[40] In both cases there are indications that the remnants of the earlier Celto-Iberian and Visigothic populations may have been scarce even before the conquest and became more so as a result of the flight of residents in the course of the wars of the Muslim conquest.

One can recognize many similarities between these *ṯuġūr* zones and the Marches in the northwestern European world, and especially the Marca (vulgo: marcha) Hispanica that from the eighth century on constituted a Christian counterpart to the Muslims' border districts. Like the Muslim ṯuġūr, the term 'marca' as used in this sense tended to imply not only an ethnic but commonly also a religious boundary: 'marca paganorum' is not an uncommon phrase.

---

[40] Bosch Vilá, J., *Albarracîn Musulman*, vol. I in: *Historia del Albarracin y de su Sierra*, M. Almagro ed. (Teruel, 1959).

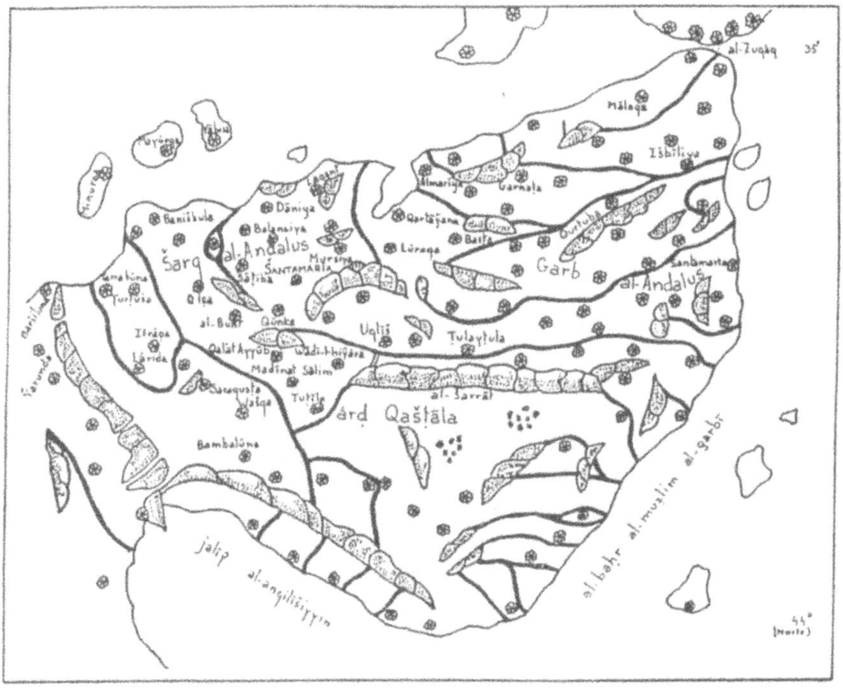

FIGURE 1.9. Copy of the parts of maps IV-1 and V-1 from al-Idrisi's Book of Roger of 1154 AD, showing the configuration of the Iberian Peninsula. The map shows very clearly the range of imaginary mountains labeled *al-šarrāt* running just south of Toledo (*Tulaytula*) E–W across much of the Peninsula.

Considering this sequence, it is clear that from the seventh well into the eleventh century in al-Andalus the concept of *ṯuġūr* derived from military realities, reflecting a long period of dynamic warfare ranging for several centuries over a relatively restricted depth of territory, and that, as a designation of geographic reality, the term designates a militarized zone of variable width, from about fifty to several hundred miles in depth (Figs. 6 and 8a), appropriate to the kind of mounted warfare typical of the time and constituting effectively a no-man's land,

أبياض الأرض ,

the 'white' (i.e., waste) lands, the 'terrae desertae' of the Castilians, and—whether sparsely or more densely populated—studded with fortresses, and at intervals marked by more important fortress towns that served as sally ports or as refuges for the warriors engaged in the actual fighting.[41]

---

[41] Cf. eg. Bosch-Vilá, J., "Consideraciones sobre al-ṯaghr en el-Andalus y la división politico-administrativa de la España" in: *Études d'orientalisme dediées à la mémoire de Lévi-Provençal*, vol. 1. (Paris, 1962), 20–33.

Ṯuġūr in the Texts of the Arabo-Islamic Geographers

Geographers recognized the distinction between the singular, *ṯaġr*, and the plural *ṯuġūr*, designations, respectively, for a zone[42] and for a town in such a zone and exercising the functions of a *ṯaġr*. Examples of the distribution of localities so designated are shown in Figure 1.7 (junction between the Byzantine Empire [including Armenia] and Syria and *al-jazīra* and compare with Fig. 1.6), Figure 1.10 (between Muslim al-Andalus and the Christian kingdoms on the Iberian Peninsula, compare with Figure 1.8), Figure 1.11 (the eastern border of the Khurasan),[43] and between Upper Egypt and the Nuba kingdom. The distribution of these fortress towns frequently suggests a line of defense or offense some distance inside of what constituted the actual lands claimed by Muslim rulers, that is, well within the *ṯuġūr* and, at least in the Syrian region and in that of al-Andalus, just outside the *'awāṣim*.

The geographers' usage of these terms can be deduced from an examination of the texts (Table 1.3): in the works of 18 geographers I found a total of 37 towns listed as *ṯaġr*, and 8 *ṯuġūr* were mentioned as districts. These data, grouped according to author, are summarized in Table 1.2; the towns named as *ṯaġr* are shown in the first thirty-seven rows, and the *ṯuġūr* in the last eight. The several numbered columns correspond to the various authors, and a key to those numbers is shown on the right of the table proper. Examination of the table as a whole suggests that use of the terms was by no means universal; on the average each author designated as *ṯaġr* fewer than 3.6 ± 3.4 localities out of a total of 35; seventeen of the eighteen authors mention towns designated as *ṯaġr*, but only seven out of eighteen mention any districts designated as *ṯuġūr*. There is no indication that either towns or districts of this kind were mentioned more frequently over the period covered by this survey.

It is clear from these observations that both the singular and the plural terms marked concepts familiar to the geographers but were hardly viewed as of overriding importance. Al-Idrisi appeared to be the least concerned with boundaries of this kind. He used the term only in reference to a single place, in regard to the 'lands beyond the river' at the eastern end of the Khurasan. His reluctance to underscore the hostile relations between Islam and Christianity is understandable considering that as a Muslim by birth, training, and faith, he wrote under the aegis and at the court of a Norman king who had fought the Muslims in North Africa and who played a major role in establishing Christian rule, albeit of an extraordinarily tolerant cast, in Sicily.

To round out the geographers' picture of the zone referred to as the *ṯuġūr* Table 1.2 showed fortresses named as lying in one such defensive zone (*ṯuġūr* and *'awāṣim*) by three geographers, one writing near the hayday of the Khalifate, one right before the Mongol invasions, and one

---

42 Ibid., p. 39.

43 For example, Ibn Ḥauqal: ṯuġūr at-turuk . . . mā warā, 'n-nahr . . . on the extreme frontier (*ḥadd*) of Islām.

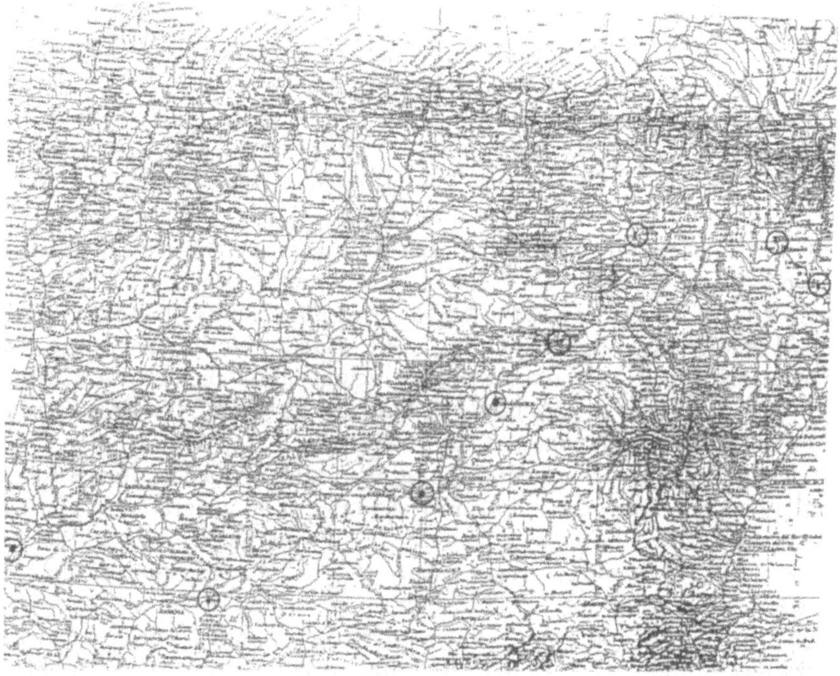

FIGURE 1.10. Modern map of part of the Iberian Peninsula showing location of towns referred to as *ṯagr* in Arabo-Islamic geographical texts. The Mediterranean Sea is shown in the lower right hand corner, and the Bay of Biscay runs over much of the top from left to right. Barcelona is just off the map on the right, and Lisbon on the left.

before the establishment of the Ottoman Empire, respectively.[44] That summary illustrates the concept of the zone of the *ṯuġūr* as a true military one, studded with fortifications of diverse sizes. Whether Table 2 implies recognition of a change in the defenses with the course of time can hardly be determined from the available data.

Summary of First Section

To recapitulate the principal result of the foregoing examination of the manner in which the two kinds of boundaries are represented in texts and cartography of the medieval Arabo-Islamic period, one can hardly do better than to cite the great fourteenth century Muslim historian Ibn Khaldun. He summed up his discussion of the overall result of the events associated with the formation of Muslim states in a passage of his Muqaddimma:[45]

..... فحيث نفد عددهم فالطرف إلذي إنتهى عنده هو ألثغر
ويحيط بألدولة من سائر جهات كالنطاق.

---

[44] Cf. Honigmann, E., EI-1, vol. 8, article *ṯuġūr*, p. 739.

[45] إبن خلدون، كتاب ألعبر، بيروت مجلد ۱، ص.٥٢٧

FIGURE 1.11. Modern map showing region of Khorasan and Bokhara, with black circles indicating towns described as *ṯuğūr* in the geographical texts.

or in F. Rosenthal's translation:[46] ". . . wherever their (warriors') numbers reach, their advance comes to a stop at (what is called) the 'border region' [F.R.'s translation of 'thaghr']. This surrounds each dynasty on all sides like a belt."

Taken together, data here assembled support the view that Arabo-Islamic geographers, while recognizing the concept of boundaries as such, did not accept the idea that these were sharply defined boundary lines separating either, as internal boundaries, one Muslim state from the

[46] Ibn Khaldun, *The Muqaddimah*, F. Rosenthal trans. (New York, NY, 1958), vol. 2, p. 125.

Table 1.3. Fortresses in *Ṯuġūr aš-Šāmīa* Listed by Three Arabo-Islamic Geographers

Region	Fortress	al-Istakhri 908 AD	ad-Dimishqi 1225 AD	al-Qalqashandi 1387 AD
Ṯ. aš-Šāmīa	Mar'aš	x	x	
	Ṭarsuṣ	x	x	x
	Aḏāna	x	x	x
	al-Masīsa	x	x	
	al-Ḥarūnīa	x	x	
	Sīs		x	x
	Aīas		x	x
	al-Kan.suada			x
	Aīn zurba	x		
	Sirfanakar			x
	ar-Rāḥa			x
	Qal'a Ja'bar			x
Ṯ. al-Jazirmīa	Malatīa	x	x	x
	Kamākh		x	
	Ṣimšāt		x	
	al-Birah		x	
	Hiṣn		x	
	Manṣūr			
	Qal'a ar-Rūm		x	
	Hadāṭ al-Hamrā'	x	x	
	Dalwagi			x
	Daranda			x
	Abulustān			x

next – deemphasized as a logical consequence of the concept of the 'umma of all believers – or, as external boundaries, Muslim from non-Muslim territory, a consequence of the mandate of the Holy War and the implied fluidity of a frontier determined by the fortunes of war. Instead, in both cases they appear to have thought in terms of a more or less extensive zone separating two realms, with a gradual transition of administrative power from one ruler to the other (cf. Fig. 1.12a and b, and note below[47]).

[47] As a *hypothesis* to account for the observations regarding the boundaries of medieval Muslim states I suggest that, in contrast to the situation for modern territorial states, in medieval Muslim political entities the situation should be described by what might be termed the 'sovereignty-field' model. The intensity of sovereignty, سيادة = siyâda or sultâna, both in terms of power and of self-identification of the subjects, is to be conceived of as being maximal and relatively constant over a region centered in its capital and the territories immediately adjacent to it. Beyond this zone, intensity of sovereignty is conceived of as radiating in all directions, diminishing with increasing distance from the capital according to some such function as the logarithmic falling-off of the intensity of the electromagnetic field around a conductor carrying a current, or the density of the atmosphere as one ascends above the earth's surface. Frontiers in such a system would correspond to regions where the intensity of sovereignty of one political unit had decreased sufficiently to be overlaid by the field of sovereignty of a neighboring unit, the intensity of which in turn would rise gradually as one approached the political center of that second entity, to peak at it's capital district (cf. Fig. 4.1).

A boundary, in such a model, could not be a sharp line. In its place one would expect boundary zones of the kind characteristic of the medieval Islamic realm as described in the

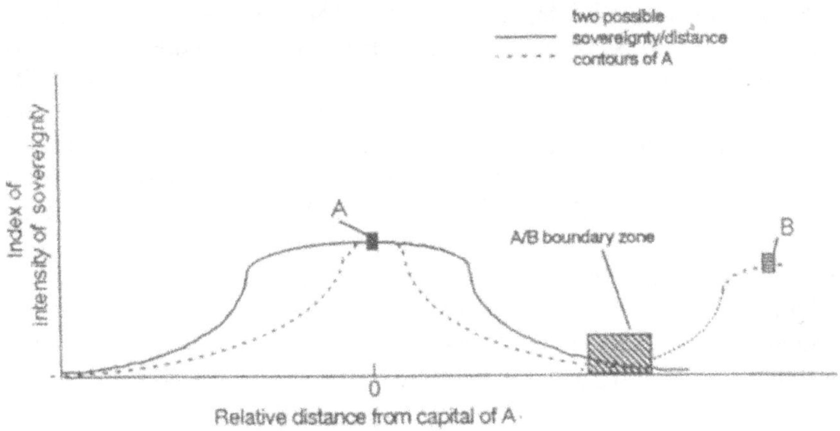

FIGURE 1.12a. Hypothetical relation of intensity of sovereignty to distance from the capital cities of two states, A and B, and their relation to the boundary zone between them.

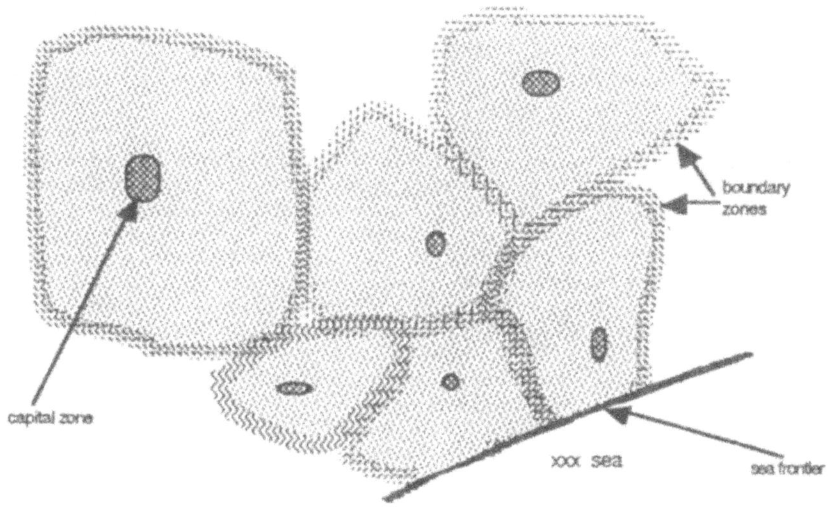

FIGURE 1.12b. Map to illustrate the relations between states conforming to the hypothetical relations illustrated in Fig. 12a.

Such a view differed from that held by the Romans. It persisted not only over the 350 years of existence of an effective khalifate, but beyond this well into the fourteenth century in spite of vast changes in the political structures of the governments that prevailed over the enormous expanse of the Islāmic realm. Such endurance of an important geopolitical manifestation would seem necessarily to reflect peculiarities of the Islāmic civilization of the Middle Ages.[48] Validation of the basic concept in terms of the experience of individuals other than the scholars who have monopolized the discussion to this point, and inquiry into the extent to which this characteristic of Arabo-Islamic geography can be understood as reflecting basic tenets of the society will occupy the next section of this essay.

Appendix
Constitutional implications of the proliferation of states during the Late Khalifate

Despite the emergence of the successor states there is no indication that the primary task of the Islamic state had changed from that envisioned by Muhammad: the state was the vehicle that assured that the Muslim could live a life in accordance with the dictates of his religion—all other functions of the state were considered subordinate to this mandate.[49] Early on, the Muslim sub-

---

preceding sections of this essay (and, incidentally, as conforming to the general view advanced by Hourani). Such zones would be expected to coincide with the portion of the curves of Figure 1-12a where the intensities of sovereignty of both neighbors would be low and change slowly with displacement on the ground. The width of such boundary zones would be determined by the actual parameters of the two curves describing the relative intensities of each of the two sovereignties in the region where their curves intersect, parameters that may well have varied from one political unit to the next as well as from time to another (these relations are illustrated in Figure 1.12a in terms of two alternative hypothetical sovereignty contours for unit A; the crosshatched area marks a possible boundary zone). In the two-dimensional map comprising a number of political units (Fig. 1-12b) such a model yields a mosaic of sovereignty fields surrounded by boundary zones between each pair of adjoining powers. Incidentally, this figure emphasizes that the fraction of the total area of a given entity that falls into boundary belt is substantially larger—and its relative importance greater—than might have been inferred from consideration of the ratio of the linear dimensions of boundary and core zones.

This hypothesis implies that precisely positioned boundary lines were omitted from the geographers' statements not by arbitrary choice, but on the basis of a knowledge of the actual conditions prevailing in the medieval Islamic realm. The picture of a central capital area surrounded by a zone of increasingly faint identification with the central zone's sovereignty corresponds very well with the pattern of representation of such units in al-Idrisi's maps (Fig. 1.5): the central core of each polity is indicated, but the frontier is left blank, reflecting the low gradient of the sovereignty-distance relation in the border zone. Similarly, the rarity of border experiences of travelers to be discussed in Section 2 now follows logically from perception of the variability of the intensity of sovereignty over its territory. Scholars holding the sort of concept proposed here would find such a view of the matter to conform well with their almost universal tendency to describe a country in terms of its capital and major cities.

[48] Maurice Lombard in his *l'Islam dans sa première grandeur* (Flammarion, Paris, 1971) has made a case for one aspect of this, the astonishing commercial network that arose following the establishment of the Islāmic Empire.

[49] Primacy of religious function of imám.

TABLE 1.4. Terms Used in Medieval Arabo-Islamic Literature Relating to the State, the Ruler, and the Subjects

The ruler	The subject	The entity
khalifa	sākin (resident)	sha'b (first step in genealogies)
sultān	haḏarī ('Anwohner')	daula (dynasty)
malik	muwaṭan ("native")	wilāya (sovereign power)
'amir	– –(XIX cent.)	waṭ'an (homeland)
		mulk (kingdom)

". . . the term 'citizen' with its connotation of the right to participate in . . . the conduct of government was totally outside the Muslim political experience . . . and therefore unknown in Islamic political language."

Bernard Lewis–*The Political Language of Islam*

ject was bound to the state primarily by his obedience to the ruler as the imām, the leader in war and at prayer. There could be only one such leader, and thus no conflicts could arise in the loyalties of a subject. As the empire grew in size and complexity this situation could not endure: religious schisms as well as the proliferation of increasingly independent functionaries heralded the progressive fragmentation of the empire described above. In view of the close link between religion and the conduct of secular affairs under Islām it was inevitable that such a situation would call for extensive reevaluation of the philosophical and constitutional basis of the Islāmic polity.

Two problems, in particular, were at the core of the ensuing attempts at clarification: the problem posed by the existence of more than one imām, and the problem of the position of the secular leader, the sultān, in the schema of things.

One can follow the progressive breakup of the Empire in terms of this literature: early on it was affirmed that there could be only one Imām–the khalifa of the Prophet–whose task was to assure that the sharī'a, the God-given Holy Law, was observed throughout his domains. Executive power could be delegated by the incumbent to a hierarchy of functionaries of descending degrees of power (four such are recognized by al-Mawardi: power over all affairs of the entire realm; power over specified affairs in all of the realm; power over all affairs in parts of the realm; and power over specified affairs in a designated part of the realm).[50] Over the years this position changed progressively:[51] there came recognition of the possibility that there could indeed be more than one imām at a given time on the condition, at first, that the two permitted imāms were separated by the sea, later on "that the seats of the several imāms were sufficiently distant from one another."

There was also a shift in the theoretical view taken of the holders of secular power, from an initial position that saw in them mere functionaries of the khalifa, through an intermediate stage in which the functionaries could perform their duties independently but only if they acknowledged the suzerainty of the khalifa,

[50] al-Mawardi, categories of functionaries.

[51] cf. Lambton, A.K.S., *State and Government in Medieval Islam* (Oxford, 1981), chapters IV to XI for extensive presentation of the progression: from Abu Yusuf (d. 798 p.e.), through al-Baqillani (d. 1013) and al-Baghdadi (d. 1038 p.e.), to al-Mawardi (972–1058 p.e.), and from him through al-Juwayni (1028–1105 p.e.) and al- Ghazali (1058–1111 p.e.) to ar-Razi (d. 1209 p.e.) and Ibn Taymiya (1262–1328 p.e.), to finish the development in the writings of Ibn Khaldun (1332–1406 p.e.).

to a final position—attained when the khalifa had been physically eliminated by the Mongols—when the sultan, the holder of 'sultān', the secular power, was recognized as the head of an independent state who might or might not also perform the functions of the imām for his subjects. This position had been prepared ever since al-Ghazālī proclaimed that the degree of peace and civic orderliness required for observance of an individual's religious duties could be assured only by the existence of an effective ruler, and that this role so far predominated over all others that legalists could enunciate the maxim: "Obey whoever is the ruler, regardless of whether he is pious and lives a good life or whether he is sinful—the burden of his sins is upon him and not the subjects."[52]

It is significant that even while these discussions progressed among the learned classes, there are indications that as far as the general public was concerned, they continued to perceive their first loyalty to their religion and its leader—or to the leader of a particular one among the more than a dozen sects into which Islām was divided by the thirteenth century—and felt little attachment to whatever dynasty happened to rule the land they lived in at the moment. Indeed, the political terminology of the period does not include any term that conveys an idea analogous to the modern concept of 'citizenship' (cf. Table 1.4), leading a prominent Islamologist to conclude: "The term citizen with its connotation of the right to participate in . . . the conduct of government was totally outside the Muslim political experience . . . and therefore unknown in Islamic political language."[53] The ordinary Muslim inhabitant of the realm was a 'subject' (ra'iya, literally herd) of a ruler, not a citizen of a state, and his loyalty to the local dynasty was weak or non-existent unless some specific oath or vow had been extracted from him in response to some specific benefit or unless he was a member of some of the categories of people who owed loyalty to the dynasty as a matter of ascription.[54] Clearly this would have been a factor rendering boundaries between Muslim states with Muslim subjects on both sides of little importance in the lives of common people.

---

52 al-Ghazālī, obedience to the sinful ruler.

53 Lewis, B., *The Political Language of Islam* (University of Chicago Press, 1988).

54 Cf. Mottahedeh, r.p., *Loyalty and Leadership in an Early Islamic Society* (Princeton University Press, 1980).

SECTION 2

Travelers' Experiences at Internal Boundaries, the Area Concept in Arabo-Islamic Geography, and the Relation of Zone-Boundaries to Basic Tenets of Arabo-Islamic Culture

The first section of this essay established that medieval Muslim geographers and historians thought of frontiers in terms of boundary zones rather than of sharply defined line boundaries. Does this sense of gradual transition from one state within the Muslim Empire to the next correspond to the perceptions of the ordinary people of the time? To answer this question we shall next examine the reports of travelers who visited these lands in medieval days.

Boundaries in the Writings of Travelers in the Islāmic Empire

Sea frontiers, unlike most other kinds, were recognized as sharply defined borders.[55] For this reason the experiences of travelers arriving by ship provide an appropriate basis for comparison with experiences associated with the crossing of zone type boundaries on land. Cargo and passengers carried on ships entering port from stations outside the jurisdiction of a given ruler were inevitably assumed to be coming from abroad.[56] All arriving passengers were subjected to sometimes highly invasive examination. Customs charges—mukūs, and later on simply ʿūshr (1/10), or still later (under the Seljuks[57]) k̲umr (1/5)—could amount for non-muslims to as much as 20 percent of the value of any goods carried. In addition, Muslim passengers were expected to carry certificates of having paid the stipulated religious dues in their place of departure, while non-Muslim d̲immis had to prove previous payment of jizīa, the head tax. Subjects of non-Muslim countries proposing to visit any part of Dār al-Islām were obliged to possess or obtain a certificate of amān from a responsible Muslim subject of the country to which they proposed to travel.[58]

Such customs revisions are documented for the port of Alexandria by Ibn Jubaîr in the eleventh century[59] as well as by Ibn Battuta for the

---

[55] Cf. e.g., al-Mawardi on sea frontiers.

[56] Khadduri, M., *The Islamic Law of Nations* (Baltimore, MD, 1966), 21; and Gibb, L.A.R., "Al-Mawardi's theory of the Khilafa," *Islamic Culture* 12 (1937): 291-302.

[57] Yusuf, M.D., *Economic Survey of Syria during the 10th and 11th Centuries* (Berlin, 1985), 120.

[58] Hatschek, J., *Der Mustamin* (Berlin, 1919); and Wansbrough, J., "The Safe-conduct in Muslim Chancery Practice," *Bull. Sch. Oriental and African Studies*, 34 (1971): 20-35.

[59] Ibn Jubaîr, abû 'l-husain muhammad, *Rihla* (Beirut, 1984), 35-36.

fourteenth,[60] for Akka (while in the hands of the crusaders) in the eleventh;[61] for Tripoli/east;[62] for Qusair and al-Tur,[63] for Aidhab and for Jidda.[8,64] For Jidda on the Sea of Qulzum we have the additional statement of the eleventh century traveler Nasir Khusrau that he was exempted from the payment of the usual dues because he had been introduced to the local governor as a jurist and a scholar, and that official in turn wrote a letter to the governor of Mecca recommending that there, too, this scholar/pilgrim should be excused from the customary payments.[65] These, then, represent the normal and expected experiences of travelers passing sharply defined external borders.[66]

By contrast, I have encountered no reports of this kind of border control in connection with overland travel anywhere within the Islamic realm. Circumstantial travel accounts that did mention the author's difficulties in passing the authorities of ports invariably fail to mention any similar experiences at boundaries passed in the course of inland travel within the Islamic realm. Examples are Ibn Jubaîr's *Rihla* (only a short section of which—the stretch between al-Madina and Damascus—involved travel with the hajj caravan and hence would have been spared any customs interference at that time),[67] Nasir Khusrau's *Safar nam-ī*,[68] Ibn Battuta's *Rihla*,[69] al-Mas'udi's *Muruj adh-dhahab*[70] and *Kitab al-Tanbih*,[71] in scattered places in Ibn Ḥauqal's *Kitāb ṣuratu 'l'arḏ*,[72] and Benjamin[73] of Tudela's *Itinerary*. Customs charges were reported on occasion as having been collected at the gates of cities well removed from any frontier, or within the administrative district of such cities, rather than at what might have constituted the border between two political entities.[74] Thus, customs collecting stations along routes on land or on the Nile are mentioned for places along routes of travel by river or on land within the territory of Egypt—in Ikhmîm[72] (p. 149), in Asuan,

---

[60] Ibn Battuta, abû 'abd allah muhammad, *Rihla* (Beirut, 1964), 29.

[61] Ibn Jubaîr, abû 'l-husain muhammad, *Rihla* (Beirut, 1984), 277.

[62] Yusuf, M.D., *Economic Survey of Syria during the 10th and 11th Centuries*, 121.

[63] Björkman, W., *Encyclopedia of Islam I*, vol. V, pp. 176–177.

[64] Nasir Khusrau, "The Safar Namih," trans. M. Nakai, Ph.D. Thesis, U. of Tennessee, Knoxville, Tenn., 1979, pp. 56, 59, 66, 70, 149, 150, 151.

[65] I have not been able to find corresponding travelers' accounts for either Mediterranean or Atlantic ports of al-Andalus although clearly a considerable volume of commercial traffic must have moved through them; cf. e.g., S.M. Imamuddin, *Muslim Spain 711–1492 A.D.* (E.J. Brill, Leiden, 1981), 130 ff.

[66] Rivers and mountain ranges might also constitute natural and sharply defined boundaries: Bartold, V.V., Preface to: *Hudūd al-alām*, trans. V. Minorsky (London, 1970), p. 42

[67] Ibn Jubaîr, Riḥla (Beirut, 1954).

[68] The Safar Namih, *Travel Journal of the Persian Nāsir Khusrau*, trans. M. Nakhai (Knoxville, Tenn, 1979).

[69] Ibn Battuta, *Rihla* (Beirut, 1964).

[70] al-Mas'udi, *muruj adh-dhahab wa-ma'ādin al-jauhar* (Beirut, 1976).

[71] al-Mas'udi, *Kitāb al-tanbih wa-'l-Ishrāf* (Leiden, 1967).

[72] Ibn Ḥauqal, *Kitāb ṣuratu 'l'arḏ* (Beirut, 1992).

[73] Goitein, S.D., *A Mediterranean Society* (Berkeley, Cal., 1988), vol. 1, p. 61; and Yusuf, M.D., *Economic Survey of Syria during the 10th and 11th Centuries*, 118.

[74] Tudela, Benjamin of, *Itinerary*, M.N. Adler trans. (London 1907).

4 farsah from the land of Nubia; and, in Mamluk times, in the village of Qatīa deep in Mamluk territory and not far from present-day Suez, on goods in passage between Egypt to Syria;[75] in Northern Syria Aleppo—a collecting station for customs in passage between Syria, Asia Minor and Diar Bakr, Egypt, and 'Iraq[76]—and Manbij;[72] in the Awāṣim of the Jazira (Akhlât[71]); in Ifriqiya-Ajdābia near Barqa in present-day Libya where 'taxes on caravans traveling from or to the Countries of the Blacks south of the Sahara were collected by the imām who presided at the Friday prayers';[77] and in the Yemen- Khamdân.[72] Other instances of episodes akin to border experiences but taking place at some distance from any actual frontier include mention by Ibn Jubair of fortified inns on the flanks of the Lebanon mountains;[78] revision of bara'a, the certificates of payment of the jizīa needed by dhimmis crossing customs stations of Muslim countries;[79] the case of a caravan pilfered (near Balis on way to Malatiya) by Hamdani military authorities;[80,81] and perhaps an episode of prisoner of war exchange on Lamis island 35 miles from Tarsus.[82] The one instance of what at first glance might bespeak a true frontier *line* experience is a passage regarding the mores of robber bands on the Frankish side between Damascus and Acre in Ibn Jubair's *Rihla*,[83] but the distinctly non-official character of the actors involved serves rather to underscore the conclusion that such sharply defined boundary points in general did not correspond to the ideas of the authorities.

Taken together, this information—or rather the sparseness thereof—regarding customs and custom houses, confirms the conclusion that, while such institutions existed and functioned in many of the ports of the Levant, of Egypt, and of Ifriqiya, comparable accounts for travel on land are remarkably scarce. When they do occur they refer almost invariably to experiences in cities at some distance from any conceivable border crossing.

---

[75] Ibn Battuta, abû 'abd allah muhammad, *Rihla* (Beirut, 1964), 55.

[76] Yusuf, M.D., *Economic Survey of Syria during the 10th and 11th Centuries*, 135.

[77] Ibn Ḥauqal, Abu al-Qasim Muhammad, *Kitāb ṣuratu 'l'arḍ* (Beirut, 1992) 166; and Lopez, R.S. and I.W. Raymond, *Medieval Trade in the Mediterranean World* (New York, 1990), 52.

[78] Ibn Jubaîr, abû 'l-husain muhammad, *Rihla* (Beirut, 1984), 228.

[79] Goitein, S.D., *A Mediterranean Society*, vol. 1, p. 62 and II, p. 384.

[80] Ibn Ḥauqal, *Kitāb ṣuratu 'l'arḍ* (Beirut, 1992), 166.

[81] al-Mas'udi, Abu 'l-hasan, *'Alî Kitāb al-tanbīḥ wa'l-išāf*, trans. Carra de Vaux (Paris, 1896), 259.

[82] Ibid.

[83] Ibn Jubaîr, abû 'l-husain muhammad, *Rihla* (Beirut, 1984), 273: ". . . then, early in the morning we resumed our travel (on the way from Damascas) to the town of Bânias. Halfway there we came across a huge oak tree of enormous bulk. We learned that this was known as the 'tree of equity' (*šajārat al-mīzān*). When we asked about the meaning of this we were told: "This is the boundary between safety and danger (literally 'confidence and fear') on this route, because of the Frankish freebooters. They murder and cut throats of whomever they catch beyond this (tree) on the Muslim side, even by only a fathom or a span beyond it; whoever is found on the Frankish side of it is made to continue his way. This is a rule among them, one of the best and the strangest among those of the Franks."

Thus, such evidence as we have been able to draw from the representation of customs institutions in the several traveler's accounts supports the thesis that, apart from sea frontiers, sharply defined boundary lines within the Islāmic Empire were either non-existent or of little practical importance—a conclusion that is well in accord with the geographers' texts and cartography. In Spuler's words: "There were no signs in the border area that the traveler was approaching or had already crossed a border from one Muslim country to another."[84]

The Concept of Area in Muslim Geographic Thought

Line boundaries serve to define the extent of the territory of a state and hence its area. In view of this, the neglect of the boundary concept in the Arabo-Islamic geographic literature finds its reflection in the absence of any perception of 'area' as a sharply quantifiable concept in Arabo-Islamic geography—both as a descriptive term on which comparisons might be based, and as an operant concept forming the basis of compound expressions, such as might provide a measure of intensity of some other parameter (e.g., population density, or yield of grain per acre as a measure of the productivity of land).

It is probably no accident that, with the exception of the single example of the azâla (a grossly asymmetric unit-100 by 1 dhirʿa, used in ʿAbbassid times as a measure of the size of irrigation canals) the names of units of area in the medieval Muslim literature and presumably the units themselves are of Persian and Egyptian origin: the Egyptian fadân, sahm, yarâd and the Sassanian jarīb and qabiz[85] (the ʿašr—though a term derived from arabic 10—as a measure is 1/10 of the Sassanian jarīb).

The Arabo-Islamic geographers themselves made no use of the concept of area.[86] When they wished to indicate the size of a country or a province they gave linear measurements of length and breadth. In the works of more than thirty medieval Muslim geographers I have not found any reference to what might seem the most natural next step, that of multiplying those two dimensions to provide an estimate of surface area for whatever entity had been described. This, of course, does not imply that such a concept was unfamiliar to the mathematicians of the period. It does mean, however, that in describing real lands, or even real structures, the people of the time made little or no use of the concept of length to the second power. Thus, while area measurements were familiarly used in Sassanid Persia and in Byzantine Egypt, in the tenth century the Persian Nasir Khusrau refers in his travel account only once

---

[84] Spuler, B., *Trade in the Eastern Islamic Countries in the Early Centuries* in: D.S. Richards, *Islam and the Trade of Asia* (Oxford, 1970), p. 11.

[85] Hinz, W., *Islamische Masse und Gewichte* (Leiden 1970), 65-66.

[86] Brauer, R.W., "Geography in the Medieval Muslim World," *Comp. Civilizations Rev.* 26 (1992): 73-110.

or twice in explicit terms to the area of a city or a building, while reporting "length and breadth" of such elements many times over.[87]

Here again, the facts as reflected in the texts are such as correspond to the zone-type of boundary encountered in the geographic literature: real lands are not conceived of as sharply circumscribed areas marked out on the surface but rather as domains of sovereignty of a ruler, commonly reported in the fashion that elsewhere I have termed "the linear concept of geography" that is, as regions transected by intersecting routes of travel and marked by scattered towns connected by such routes.

Land Tax Data as the Basis for Quantifying the Area of a Political Entity

As an alternative to recognizing explicitly the concept "area of a political unit" as an abstract but quantifiable concept deducible from linear measurements on the ground, one might consider deriving an equivalent sense from fiscal data. Thinking of a given province as made up of a number of small parcels of individually held or worked land would result in the sum of their areas being a measure of the total area of that province. Encouraged by reports of Khalif ʿUmar's cadastral survey of the Sawad in Southern ʿIraq,[88] one might consider the possibility of testing such a concept on the basis of data concerning revenues derived from the land tax. In actual practice it is readily shown that such a substitute for the area concept could not have been feasible.

Because of the manner in which land ownership and the associated tax liabilities were conceived, it is the ḵarāj collected from the lands farmed by ḏimmis that is of concern here.[89] Thus, the matter becomes

---

87 Nasir Khusrau, "The Safar Namih," trans. M. Nakai, Ph.D. Thesis Univ. of Tennessee, Knoxville, Tenn., 1979.

88 al-Mawardi, Abou 'l-Hasan, *Les Statuts Gouvernementaux*, trans. E. Fagnan (Algiers, 1915), p. 370–372. Note, however, that more recent indications suggest that such surveys as did take place produced data that seem incompatible with the actual dimensions of the lands supposedly surveyed.

89 In the desert lands of the Arabian Peninsula as well as among the sedentary oasis populations within the original heartlands of Islam, the concept of taxing land holdings (and indeed the concept of individual ownership of land) was but slightly developed. Whatever land tax was exacted from the oasis dwellers in pre-Islamic times was based on agricultural production, computed as a fraction of the amount or value of each kind of produce harvested rather than on the basis of the area worked, and it was paid more in kind than in cash. Early land revenue measures enunciated by the Prophet Muhammad (F. Løkkegaard, *Islamic Taxation in the Classical Period* (Copenhagen 1950), p. 185ff; and Chelhod, J., *Le droit dans la société bédouine* (Paris, 1971, c. 8) were based on the principle that within the realm of Islam all land belonged to God and, by delegation, to the community of believers, and hence was not taxable as such (Løkkegaard, F., *Islamic Taxation*, c. 1). This idea was firmly established for the sacred lands of the Arabian Peninsula and also accompanied the victorious Arabic troops on their conquests: Arabs were not to be subject to any taxation related to their ownership of land, but neither were they to be directly involved at this stage with any aspect of agricultural use of the newly dominated lands—a matter left to the increasing numbers of non-Muslims who, with the conquests, came under the rule of the Khalifs and their successors. These clearly could not lay claim to a share in the bounty of the communal land ownership of those confessing Islam, and hence were properly the subjects of taxation related to their use of the land. It was probably under the khalifate of Muʿawīa ibn abi sufyān (661–680 AD) that these ideas were said by later writers (such as al-Mawardi) to have been incorporated into the theory of a more formal tax structure of the

relevant to the present discussion only when substantial lands tilled by non-Muslim populations came to be included in the Islāmic Empire as a result of the early conquests in the Middle East and in Egypt under Khalifs 'Umar ibn 'abd al-ḵattab and 'Uṯmān ibn 'affān. At that point the matter of taxation immediately was complicated by casuistry: as a result of the insistence of the khalifs upon the principle that soil ownership should be restricted to Muslims alone, either in the form of public lands benefiting the community of the faithful as a whole or as individuals, while yet Arabs were not supposed to till the newly conquered land,[90] non-Muslim non-Arabs had to be allowed one of several forms of usufruct under conditions determined by the terms under which their lands had been incorporated into the Islāmic Empire. Furthermore, in the Middle East, land without an assured water supply is of little value, and such as there was, was also assigned to one of several classes that affected the tax burden upon the lands served, creating further categories in the overall tax structure. In the course of time, the financial needs of the state – strained in their resources by numerous conversions that undercut the tax base (as well as by the increasing shortage of silver for its coinage) – led to the determination that transfer of land from ḏimmis to Muslims did not (or not necessarily) lift the liability to ḵarāj payments, and here again, special rulings were required to permit what had earlier been interdicted and to find a place for these payments in an increasingly bewildering tax edifice.[91]

All of this still did not establish a suitable standard for determining the basis upon which any ḵarāj to be collected should be calculated. Two alternatives are said to have been recognized as early as 639 AD by 'Umar in connection with the formulation of a taxation policy for the Sawad, the fertile "Black Lands" of the Euphrates-Tigris Delta:[92] a proportional tax based upon the product of the soil, or a tax based upon the area tilled by a given taxpayer and differentiated according to the kind of crop, قصامة and مساحة = qusāma and misāḥa, respectively.[93] 'Umar is said to have chosen to follow initially the patterns that had been applied in the region while under Byzantine and Sassanian rule prior to the Muslim conquest, and this approach became widespread in the sequel.

---

future Islamic Empire (cf. qur'an or hadith re land ownership): like most other facts of a given individual's life, his tax liability would be determined largely by his religious affiliation: tithe, عشر = 'ushr, and alms, زكة = zakat, for the Muslim; head tax, جزية = jizīa, and taxes of various kinds, including in particular the land (use) tax, jointly referred to as خراج = ḵarāj, for ḏimmis, the 'people of the book' living under the protection of Islam in Dār al-Islām.

90 Note that Hitti contends that the divisions mentioned above may be pure invention introduced post facto by Mawardi and Ibn Yunus, and that the real situation was as depicted in the next paragraphs, with minimal input of Qur'anic or later religio-political concepts (cf. ref. 32).

91 Juinboll, Th.W., in *Encyclopedia of Islam*, vol. 3, p. 901.

92 al-Mawardi, Abou 'l-Hasan 'Ali, *Les Statuts Gouvernementaux*, trans. E. Fagnan (Algiers, 1915), p. 370.

93 E.g., al-Mawardi, Abou 'l-Hasan 'Ali, *Les Statuts Gouvernementaux*, trans. E. Fagnan (Algiers, 1915), p. 312.

In essence there were three such patterns: that, already mentioned above, prevailing in the Sassanid Empire; that prevailing in the Roman Empire under Byzantine domination; and that evolved in Egypt out of the earlier post-Alexandrine and the subsequent Byzantine land tax policies. All three can be reduced to a common denominator, harking back to the tax reform undertaken under the Roman emperor Diocletian in 414 AD. This produced the compromise pattern of the "capilatio (et) iugatio" (i.e., head and acreage) taxation as the universally applicable basis of land tax structure,[94] one readily recognizable in the land tax of the Sassanian Empire (although distorted during the later days of the regime by practices such as collective assessment of whole villages or even districts) as well as being the basis on which taxation of farmers was based in Byzantine Egypt. It was this pattern that was transposed in the early Islamic structure of taxes on ḏimmis, ḵarāj and jizīa,[95] and that was the subject of elaboration and complication in the manner described.

Even this complex pattern did not endure long. Actual distribution of lands involved not only the differentiation of public lands and ḵarāj lands tilled by ḏimmis, but to an increasing extent lands given to soldiers as a reward or in lieu of payment in the form of iqtāʿa of several types—holdings that increasingly assumed a quasi-feudal character and, being held by Muslims, were subject to ʿušr—the tenth (or later, ḵums—the fifth), an impost related in effect to product rather than area of the land.[96,97]

As a result of all these tendencies, the areas of any one of the political subdivisions of the Empire, and later on of any of the several Muslim-ruled states, came to be made up of a complex mosaic of landholdings subject to a bewildering plethora of tax regimens only a small part of which corresponded to the original concept of land tilled by ḏimmīs and paying a well defined area-based (misāḥa) ḵarāj. As the financial situation of many of these political entities became increasingly precarious, the matter was still further complicated by a whole array of other charges and taxes related to the conduct of different forms of agriculture.[98] State revenue reports tended to lump these different kinds of imposts in such fashion that the figures bore little relation to area tilled or used, or to the volume of different kinds of produce harvested.[99]

The result of all these considerations is that land tax returns were apt to fluctuate wildly (cf. e.g., Ibn Ḥauqal) and did not at any time bear a unique relation to land area in cultivation or pasture. Figures for the total

---

[94] Ostrogorsky, G., *History of the Byzantine State* (New Brunswick, NJ, 1969), p. 40.

[95] *Cambridge History of Iran* 3[2], p. 746; and Hitti, P.K., *A History of Syria* (New York, 1951), p. 423.

[96] Yusuf, M.D., *Economic Survey of Syria during the 10th and 11th Centuries*, 32.

[97] Cahen, C., in *Encyclopedia of Islam II*, vol. 4, pp. 1030–1034, reports that frontier soldiers were at times allowed to substitute military service for ʿushr payments.

[98] F. Løkkegaard, *Islamic Taxation in the Classical Period* (Copenhagen 1950), 185.

[99] Examples of tax revenue lists: **Шамскочяна, А.С.- Хараджж по Арабским географам Ix-x вв.- in: Ибн ал-Факих- Ахбар ал- Булдан- Ереван,** 1979, p. 139–142, and Cahen, C., "Le régime foncier dans le Fayyoum Ayyoubide," *Arabica* 3 (1956): 12 ff.

area of any political or administrative unit were available for or from any kind of tax computation only from early times, and then only for lands such as those of Egypt and parts of the former Sassanian Empire where area-based land tax had been in use before the advent of Islam.[100]

Summing up the limited data concerning the role of "area" in describing geographical entities, we conclude that it was given little or no significance by the geographers, and that in relation to state imposts, too, it exerted remarkably little influence. It was significant, at least in theory, only in those places and in those periods where the influence of earlier empires, Byzantine or Sassanian, continued to be strongly felt, and even there its practical importance came to be overlaid by other considerations and other measures well before the end of the eleventh century. All told, these attitudes accord well with a geography in which sharp boundaries played little or no role.

Boundary Characteristics as a Consequence of Embedded Attitudes of the Culture

The data presented justify the conclusion that neglect of boundaries was not only a fact of geographical science as it was written in the Muslim empire from the eighth to the twelfth century. It also corresponded to the experience of contemporary travelers, and was at least not in conflict with the views of administrators of the period. These observations suggest that this peculiarity of Muslim geographical perception, rather than being fortuitous or determined by lack of technical resources, must reflect certain fundamental traits of the intellectual or religious culture of the Islāmic Empire. In fact, at least six aspects of the medieval Arabo-Islamic culture jointly or separately could have contributed to this result:

1. The ʿumma, the community of believers, was defined originally in purely religious terms as coherent and united by its creed—in this sense all Muslims were brothers, not separated by any internal borders within Dār al-Islām.[101] With the eclipse of the ʿAbbasid khalifate, this perception gave way in the tenth and eleventh centuries to a period of decentralization and formation of separate states within the former boundaries of the Islāmic Empire. The most widely adopted position of the jurists probably was that of al-Mawardi (974–1058)[102] who proclaimed that "only where the Islamic lands are divided by a sea (and in later views perhaps also by other natural barriers) the territory of Dâr al Islâm can the realm be conceived of as divided into two (or more) political communities the rulers of which are independent of each other though they owe ultimately subservience to the Imām." Thus, internal boundaries, at the outset were viewed as conflicting with the basic tenets of Islam; from the tenth

---

[100] For example, Cahen, C., "Le régime foncier dans le Fayyoum Ayyoubide," *Arabica* 3 (1956): 8–30.

[101] Khadduri, M., *The Islamic Law of Nations* (Baltimore, MD, 1966), 15–17.

[102] Ibid, p. 21; and Gibb, L.A.R., "Al-Mawardi's theory of the Khilafa," *Islamic Culture* 12 (1937): 291–302.

century on, such boundaries were recognized implicitly, but continued to be viewed as in a sense non-canonical (cf. Appendix to Section 1).

2. Primary function of the state, in a view universally accepted by Islamic jurists, was to assure that all Muslims could lead a life in keeping with the mandates of the Qur'an and discharge their obligations to Allah. Neither the unitary 'Umma of the seventh and eighth centuries nor the subsequently emerging political communities were territorial states[103] although, to assure the basic functioning of such entities, certain actions that have territorial consequences were prescribed for the Imām or in later times for the multiple rulers succeeding him in his secular functions.[104] In the resulting relation between the people at large and their rulers loyalties remained focused on religious aspects rather than on the dynastic or territorial claims of the state.

3. In the relations between the territories forming part of the Islamic realm and adjoining non-Islamic states, the overtly dominant role was played by the weight given to the command to engage in the jiḥād, the Holy War against the Unbeliever.[105] In the Qur'an (IX, 29) and in the opinions of the early jurists—including most notably Abu Hanifa[106]—this command mandated Holy War against the Unbeliever only when the latter threatened to interfere with the functioning of the Islamic State. By the middle of the tenth century the position had changed, and jurists from Abu Yusuf on pronounced the duty of all Muslims to wage war unremittingly against the Unbeliever until all mankind should be united in Islam.[107] While the making of temporary peace—if it was advantageous to the Muslim cause—was allowed, such peace must never last longer than ten years at a time. For the centuries before the sixteenth (when the concept of coexistence and the principle of reciprocity in international affairs came to be more widely accepted and the 'hot war' mandate came to be replaced increasingly by what Prince Juan Manuel in the thirteenth century called 'la guerra fría', 'the cold war'[108]) this mandate thus rendered the frontier between Dār al-Islām and Dār al-ḥarb, the land of war of the Unbeliever, permanently unstable and subject to the fortunes of a continuing war of offense. Later on this changed to defense, waged largely as a war of movement (although siege warfare often played an important role in the eventual outcome of these campaigns[109]).

4. Landed property, within this system, was owned exclusively by

---

103 Vaticotis, P.J., *Islam and the State* (London 1987), 30.

104 al-Mawardi, Abou 'l-Hasan, *Les Statuts Gouvernementaux*, trans. E. Fagnan (Algiers, 1915), 30-32.

105 Ibid., 31; and Khadduri, M., *War and Peace in the Law of Islam* (Baltimore, 1951). Note that this mandate by itself defined the Islamic state as a 'transcendental grouping' in the sense of Watt rather than as a state in the modern sense of the term.

106 Abu Hanīfa, an-nu'man ibn thâbit, *kitāb al- muṣnād*, ed. Safwad al-saqqa (Aleppo, 1962).

107 Cf. Lambton, A.K.S., *State and Government in Medieval Islam* (Oxford, 1980).

108 Arías, L.G., *El concepto de la guerra y la denominada 'guerra fría'* (Zaragoza, 1956).

109 Lot, F., *L'art militaire et les armées au Moyen Age en Europe et dans le Proche Orient* (Paris, 1946), vol. 1, p. 17.

Allah or, by delegation, by the Prophet and his successors, the khalifs. Man may have been granted the right of making use of the land, but it is never wholly clear whether such right of usufruct is conferred upon the community of believers as such or whether it can be held by individuals without violating some of the concepts of a strict orthodoxy.[110] The situation is further complicated by the fact that both the lands of newly occupied territories and the rights of individuals to benefit from them are not uniform but were perceived by the 'rightly guided' khalifs and in the sequel by the jurists as falling into a number of categories determined by such factors as the mode of acquisition (e.g., by force or by peace treaty), the role played by the possessor in the actual warfare leading to the acquisition of a particular stretch of land, his belonging to one or another tribal grouping, and of course his religious status as a Muslim or as a member of the protected religions, a ḏimmi.[111] As mentioned above, all these factors affected the tax liability upon the land, a matter further complicated by the fact that land in the Middle East for the most part cannot be cultivated without water rights. These, too, were subject to further categorization, special provision being made for how the land was used as for those lands not effectively utilized. Thus, the character of land tenure all but precluded any effective conception of 'territory of a state' as the essence of the identity of its citizens. Later writers who proclaimed the duty of the subject to obey whoever held power over him[112] further contributed to rendering all frontiers vague and temporary in the subjects' minds.

5. The medieval Islāmic Empire shared with most of its predecessors in the Middle East a strongly urban orientation.[113] While its soldiery was often derived from the open lands – the camel-rearing bedouin at the outset, and other non-city dwelling populations like the Turks later on – its organs of government and administration, its intelligentsia, and the repositories of its wealth were concentrated in its towns. The sedentary farmer was held in little more respect among the urban populations of the capitals than among the nomad bedouin of the heartlands: to all of these the role of the rural population was primarily that of raising the food needed to supply the cities' wants or to supplement the nomads' diet,[114] of supplying soldiers, of breeding beasts of burden, and perhaps of providing some of the caravaneers for the transport of goods between different cities. It seems inevitable that under these circumstances the projection of power over the territory of a given ruler was not uniform but rather radiated from his urban center(s) in ever diminishing intensity

---

110 F. Løkkegaard, *Islamic Taxation in the Classical Period*, c. II and III.

111 Cf. preceding paragraph and: F. Løkkegaard, *Islamic Taxation in the Classical Period*, 72–91.

112 Ya'qoub, abou yousouf, *kitābu 'l-karāj*, trans. E. Fagnan (Paris, 1921), 15; and Vaticotis, P.J., *Islam and the State* (London, 1987), 36.

113 Vaticotis, P.J., *Islam and the State*, 20.

114 Cf. Brauer, R.W., "The camel and its role in shaping mideastern nomad societies," *Comparative Civilizations Review* 28 (1993): 106–151, esp. 117–118.

as the distance from the capital towns increased. Thus, as developed in the preceding section, frontiers between Islamic states, rather than being sharp dividing lines separating adjoining political units, came to be areas where, as the power exerted by one ruler diminished to the vanishing point, the power an adjoining ruler was able to exert increased gradually from nil toward the level it might attain near the urban center of his own rule (cf. 'Hypothesis' as discussed in footnote 47 and Fig. 12).

6. In what might seem to constitute a contradiction with what was said in the preceding paragraph one must not overlook the profound influence exerted early upon Islamic political thought by the ways of the bedouin nomads of the Arabian Peninsula,[115] an influence that was pervasive especially in the field of law, and that left an indelible imprint upon the šarīʿa land–law that has never been wholly dissipated.[116] In the present context the relevant factor is the matter of territorial rights as they are claimed by all components of the segmental society of the great bedouin tribes. In a desert environment large stretches of land are worthless as such; property rights are in a sense punctate–they attach to a small piece of home land, the himā (often based merely on the right of first occupation),[117] to wells and to pasture areas. Rights may also attach to the passage of others over any part of the tribal territory, defining lines of travel that the group may close or leave open at its discretion, but such rights are largely a measure of a tribe's ability to enforce such rights militarily. None of these perceptions encourage these tribal nomads to think in terms of definite boundary lines surrounding their larger territory, although tribal memory may enshrine landmarks that help to define where a given group will claim rights on the basis of past memory.[118,119] ('. . . points that marked the limits beyond which one might reasonably expect to become the subject of hostile acts by members of a neighboring tribe'.) The nomads' point of view came with the nomad warriors of the futūh to the newly occupied territories and was reflected in the insistence by ʿUmar ibn ʿabd al-ḵattab and his successors upon the importance of communally owned lands as a significant resource of the Islamic community, worthy of being defended against excessive encroachment by lands allocated to individuals either in the form of iqtāʿa or some of the more permanent forms of usufruct analogous to the nomad himā. Here again, the overall effect of the several strictures is to render the concept of a sharply defined boundary inconsistent with the 'set' of the culture as a whole.

---

115 F. Løkkegaard, *Islamic Taxation in the Classical Period*, 20.

116 Ibid., 20.

117 Ibid., 14-37.

118 Raswan, C., "Tribal Areas and Migration Routes of North Arabian Bedouins," *Geogr. Rev.* 20: 494-502, 1951; cf. also: Stewart, F.H., *Bedouin boundaries in Central Sinai and the Southern Negev* (Brill, 1963).

119 Cf. Gulliver, P.H., *Nomadic Movements* in: Monod, T., *Pastoralism in Tropical Africa* (London, 1975), 382 regarding the absence of operating concepts of territoriality among a wide range of African and Near Eastern nomads.

All these considerations, thus, would have combined to cause Muslim scholars as well as the general public to think of boundaries, both within Dār al-Islām and between Dār al-Islām and states of Unbelievers, as vague and blurred rather than as sharp lines of demarcation. We must conclude that this state of affairs—that corresponds to what was found in the works of the geographers—is an expression of the very tenets that defined the Muslim world as one subject to the religious precepts of Islam and to all their implications for the management of political affairs.

SECTION 3

Genesis of Boundary Zones Involving non-Arab Muslim States: The Case of Asia Minor

Did Muslim imperial societies other than the Arabo-Iranian one develop against lands of Unbelievers "external boundaries" that show characteristics similar to those of the ṯuġūr of the Near East and the Iberian Peninsula?[120] The one example of the formation of an enduring empire at the gates of the Arabo-Islamic state, and that overlaps the later phases of that empire's waning, is represented by the protracted series of struggles, lasting from the tenth to the fourteenth century, at the interface between Turkish forces and the Byzantine Empire. The result was to bring about the Turkification of and the establishment of Ottoman predominance in Asia Minor. It may be significant that with the final firm establishment of Ottoman hegemony, the open and zone-type frontiers of interest here seem to have closed to become replaced increasingly by firm borders more or less on the style of the late Roman empire. This observation may well be of significance to a clearer understanding of the political meaning of such frontiers in the late medieval world.

Because of its protracted nature this situation affords a valuable study of the forces giving rise to such frontiers and the peculiar characteristics that they displayed. The Arab-led conquests of the seventh and early eighth centuries that led to the establishment of the Arabo-Islamic Empire progressed at such a rapid pace that it is difficult to unravel there the processes underlying the formation of the ṯuġūr, the marches. By contrast, the Turkification of Byzantine Asia Minor leading up to the establishment of the Ottoman Empire lasted more than 300 years from the late tenth to the fourteenth century and involved recurrent struggles between the Byzantine Empire and entities of the Turko-Muslim world. As will be shown presently, these events, like the earlier conquests, were associated with the formation of boundary zones. Because of the extended time span occupied by the events in Asia Minor, the repetitive nature of the action, and the substantial physical expanse affected, one may hope to find here a greater opportunity to analyze the interplay of the several factors underlying the development of these zones than in connection with the events of the Arabo-Islamic conquests.

---

[120] The obvious question that remains is whether similar structures were to be encountered in connection with non-Muslim societies. A subsequent essay assesses the degree of diversity of sequences leading to the formation of such geographical structures, and the social and conceptual significance that may be attached to them.

Table 3.1. A Brief Chronology of Events in Asia Minor Pertinent to Emergence of Boundary Zones at Turko/Byzantine Frontier

Date p.e.	Seljuk Turks	Other Turks	Date p.e.	Byzantium
900	begin Oghuz migration		800–1050	Byzantium counter offensive vs. Arabs
1000	begin formative stage/Seljuks			
1055	Tughril named Sultan/Baghdad	begin Turcoman incursions in east Asia Minor (1027 p.e.)		
1071	Battle of Manzikert–penetration of Turcoman raiders to shores of Aegean sea	Danishmend ghazi in Asia Minor (1060)	1097	First Crusade in Constatinople; western Asia Minor recovered by Byzantium; Comnenes.
1150	Seljuks of Rum rulers in Konia	Danishmendits eliminated (1180 p.e.)	1176	defeat by Seljuks/Myriokephalon
			1200	eastern frontier breaking up
1204	all Asia Minor under Seljuks of Rum		1204	fourth crusade sacks Constantinople; basileus moved to Nicea/Lascarids
1219–1236	Kaiqobad sultan of Seljuks at peak of their power		1204–1261	empire of Nicea; peace with Seljuks
1230	Baba Ishaq rebellion			
1243	Köse Dagh–defeat of Seljuks by Mongols	renewal of Turcoman raids on Byzantine Asia Minor (about 1245)	1261	return of Emperor to Constantinople; begin Paleologue rule
1250		begin formation of ghazi beyliks-Qaraman, Germian, Ottoman as well as (after 1280) of pirate beyliks on South and West coasts of Asia Minor	1284	dismantling of Byzantine fleet by Paleologues
1300	disappearance of Seljuks of Rum	strengthening of Ottoman State		
		1326 take Bursa		
		1331 take Nicea		
		1340 in control of all of Asia Minor	1340	all of western Asia Minor lost
		1356 victory over European knights at Nicopolis		
1400		all of ghazi beyliks in Asia Minor under Ottoman rule		
1402		Ottomans defeated at Ankara by Timur-I Lang		
1453		conquest of Constantinople by Mehmed II	1453	fall of Constantinople

The Historical Setting*

We know little about the Oghuzz, the people from whom the Seljuk took their origin in their pre-expansion domain north of the two seas. Their realm does not seem to have included any major towns. By analogy with other Turkish tribes of the period it is reasonable to surmise that their tribal elements, too, were characterized by conical tribal descent patterns and a pronounced chief-oriented organization,[121] and were made up of a mixture of sedentarized farmers and pastoral nomads, herding sheep, cattle, perhaps some two-humped camels, and especially horses.[122]

In the course of little more than fifty years one group of these Oghuzz, known to history as the Seljuks,[123] had become the masters of the largest of the Central Asian nomad empires, a realm encompassing a great portion of what had been the Islāmic Empire at its apogee and extending from Transoxania to the border of Syria, and from the latitude of Northern India to that of Georgia on the Black Sea (cf. Fig. 3.1). In the course of the centuries here under consideration the now largely Islamized tribal grouping that gave rise to the dynasty of the Great Seljuks had entered Baghdad. Its leader, Toghril ibn Muhammad, accredited by the Khalif, had taken the title of Sultan, and assumed *de facto* government of the Islamic heartlands. In doing so he had deliberately assimilated his style of rule to the forms of the urbanized and sedentarized Arabo-Iranian bureaucratic government he had found in place in the former 'Abbasid territories and adopted the manner expected of an Islamic prince (cf. Table 3.1 and Appendix to Section 3 for more complete summaries of the ensuing complex sequence of events).

By 1060 AD the Ghaznavids had been displaced from most of their remaining holdings in the Khorasan, the Qïpchaqs had advanced into the territories between the Caspian and the Aral Seas and spread for some distance to the east of there, and the Great Seljuk Empire (i.e., the empire of the Seljuk dynasty ruling in Baghdad), nearing its zenith, was impinging upon Byzantine territories in Georgia, Armenia, and Asia Minor[124] (Fig. 3.2b).

In the years following the Battle of Manzikert on the threshold of Armenia in 1071 AD, the battle in which the Byzantine emperor Romanus

---

* Cf. the Appendix to this section.

121 Barfield, T.J., "Tribe and State relations," in P. S. Khoury and J. Kostiner, *Tribe and Statehood in the Middle East* (University of California Press, Berkeley, 1990), 164 ff.

122 Cf. Roux, J.-P., "Le chameau en Asie Centrale," *Central Asiatic J.* 5 (1959): 35–76.

123 It should be noted that, while all of the Oghuzz tribes seem to have believed themselves to share a common blood line, 'tribes' of Turks in Central and Western Asia during the period here under consideration were often merely synthetic ones, the result of the gathering of warriors around some particularly astute military lèader with a tribal genealogy invented ex post facto. This was certainly the case for the Osmanlis, and probable for the Danish mendites as well as for the Seljuks. The leadership role of the chief named Seljuk in the migrations and struggles that led to the formation of the Seljuk empire is acceptably documented (cf. Cahen, C., trans. J. Jones-Williams, *Pre-Ottoman Turkey*, 19–20).

124 Bosworth, C.E., "The political and dynastic structure of the Iranian World" in: *Cambridge History of Iran*, A. Boyd ed., vol. 5. (Cambridge 1968), 298–305.

FIGURE 3.1. The Seljuk empire near the end of the eleventh century (from: C. Cahen, *Pre-Ottoman Turkey*, New York, 1968, p. 18).

IV Diogenes was defeated by Toghril's successor Alp Arslan and that opened the floodgates of Turcoman raiding into Anatolia[125] (cf. Fig. 4.3), the representatives the Seljuk dynasty had despatched to Anatolia made themselves increasingly independent of the government at Baghdad, so that from about 1110 on until about 1300 AD, while the power of the Great Seljuks was waning,[126] one can speak of the Seljuks of Rum as rulers of an independent state, waxing and waning in extent as the fortunes of war and politics changed in Asia Minor. Throughout its history this state resembled that of the Great Seljuks of the Near East in that its rulers aspired to be recognized as Islamic rulers in the full sense of the word, building mosques, making gifts, and above all ruling through a bureaucracy of Iranian style, supported by a professional army that in composition resembled the slave professional armies of Baghdad and Cairo.[127]

The almost constant warfare of the three centuries following the Seljuks' entry into the Anatolian theater—from the time of the battle of Manzikert until the rise of the Ottomans—saw the boundaries between the Byzantine and the Turkish domains swept no less than five times over large portions of Asia Minor:

---

[125] Cahen, C., trans. J. Jones-Williams, *Pre-Ottoman Turkey* (New York, NY, 1968), p. 58.

[126] Köprülü, M. Fuad, trans. G. Leiser, *The Origins of the Ottoman Empire* (Albany, NY, 1992) (orig. 1935), 43; and Cahen, C., trans. J. Jones-Williams, *Pre-Ottoman Turkey*, 103.

[127] Köprülü, M. Fuad, trans. G. Leiser, *The Origins of the Ottoman Empire*, 77.

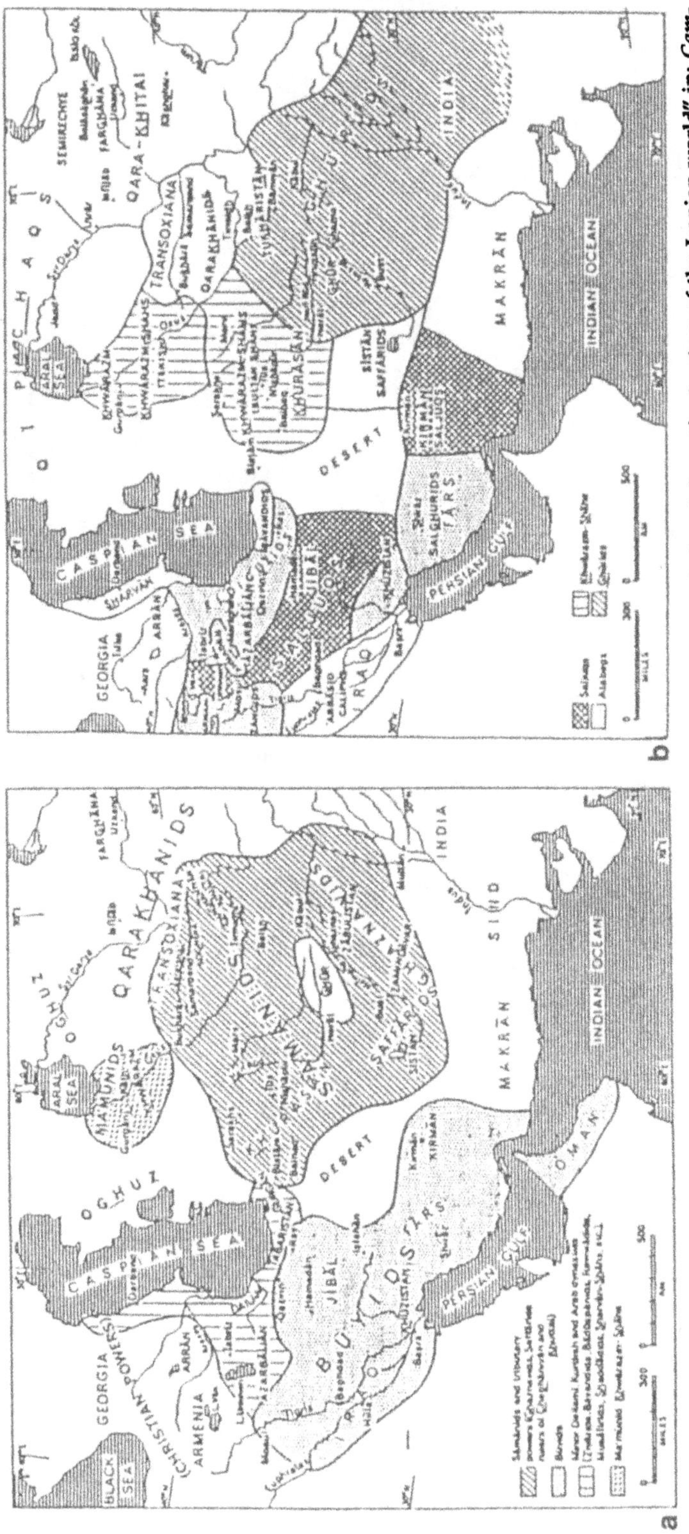

FIGURE 3.2. **The Iranian world in 998 (left) and 1180 (right), from Bosworth, C.E., "The political and dynastic structure of the Iranian world" in: *Cambridge History of Iran*, A. Boyd ed., vol. 5. (Cambridge, 1968), pp. 2 and 189.**

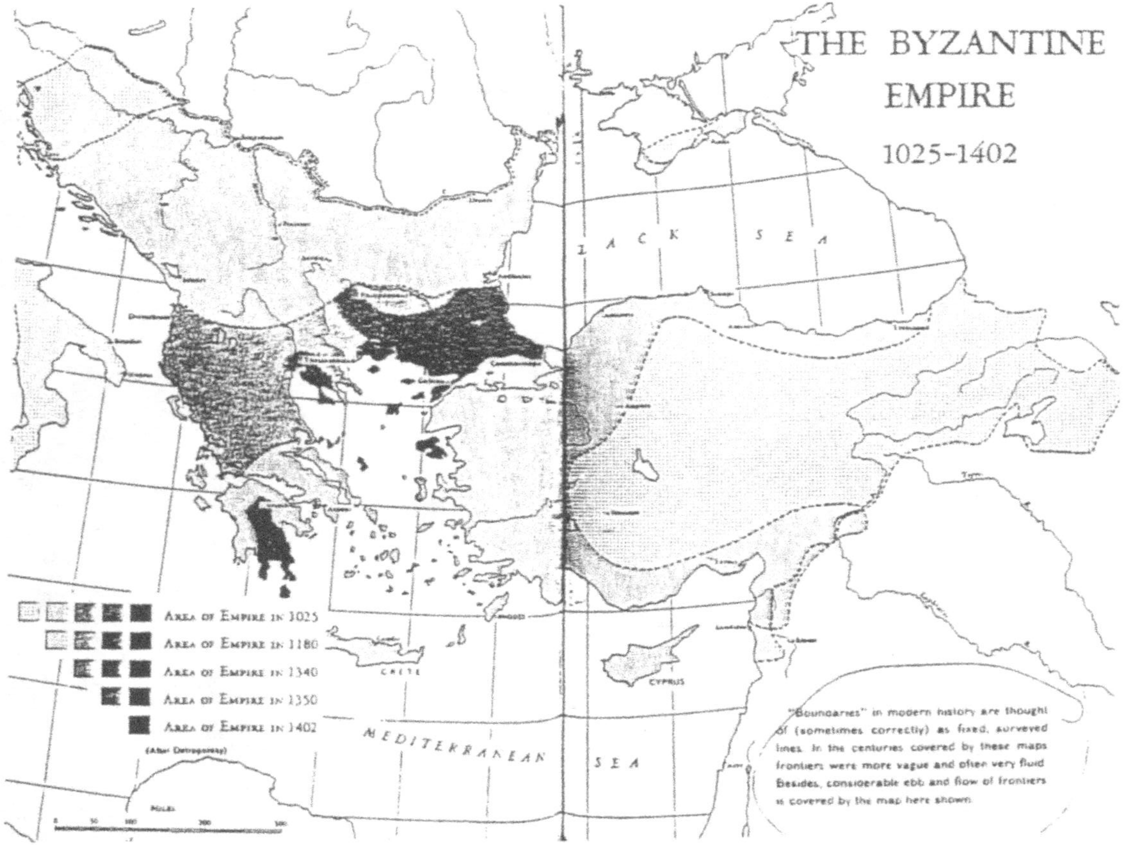

FIGURE 3.3. Successive changes in the area occupied by the Byzantine Empire, from: Vasiliev, A.A., *History of the Byzantine Empire*, vol. 1 (Madison Wisc., 1964), pp. 480–81.

1. in the initial advance of the Turks during the eleventh and early twelfth century,
2. during the recoil of the western and southern boundaries of the Turks following the first crusade,
3. in the course of the recovery and completion of the renewed conquest of western Asia Minor by the Turks in the late twelfth century,
4. as a result of the rebound of the Empire under the Lascarids in the first half of the thirteenth century and recovery by them of western and parts of central Asia Minor,
5. during the rebound—this time for good—of the Turks under Mongol pressure from the east in the second half of the thirteenth century.

In addition there were internal fights among the Turkish beyliks (Fig. 3.4), most important in the present context those that in the course of the fourteenth century led up to complete domination of the peninsula by the Osmanlis.

The Boundary Zones Associated with the Conquest of Asia Minor

The broad outlines of the geography of the successive borders between the Turkish and Byzantine-held territories are reasonably well defined and have been summarized, for instance, in the scholarly analysis of Honigmann.[128] The actual configuration of the interface between Turkish and Christian lands in Asia Minor, however, and especially in Anatolia—like that between Moorish and Christian lands in al-Andalus (cf. Fig. 1.8b)—was almost certainly much more complex. Especially during the first two centuries of the conquest, the Seljuk advances were associated with Turcoman raids that often reached deeply into Byzantine territory, leaving a mosaic of ravaged lands in which conditions approximated those characteristic of the major frontiers. No detailed data seem to exist to describe the actual distribution of the resulting fragmented boundary patches. There is, however, a consensus among the historians dealing with these events that all of the resulting boundary represented a no-man's land of some depth, rather than a front or a borderline in the modern sense. This conclusion is enunciated over and over in Wittek's work[129] as in that of Köprülü,[130] in Cahen's[131] as in Lindner's,[132] Vryonis'[133] or Kwanten's,[134] each based on numerous original sources.

These descriptions recall many aspects also characteristic of the Syrian and the Jazirīan ṯuġūr, especially in regard to the wasteland aspect of

---

[128] Honigmann, E., *Die Ostgrenze des Byzantinischen Reiches* (Bruxelles, 1935).
[129] Wittek, P., *The Rise of the Ottoman Empire* (New York, NY, 1971 [original 1938]).
[130] Köprülü, M. Fuad, trans. G. Leiser, *The Origins of the Otttoman Empire.*
[131] Cahen, C., trans. J. Jones-Williams, *Pre-Ottoman Turkey.*
[132] Lindner, R.P., *Nomads and Ottomans in Medieval Anatolia* (Bloomington, Ind., 1983).
[133] Vryonis, *The Decline of Medieval Hellenism in Asia Minor and the Process of Islamization from the Eleventh through the Fifteenth Century* (Berkeley, CA, 1971).
[134] Kwanten, L., *Imperial Nomads* (Philadelphia, PA, 1979).

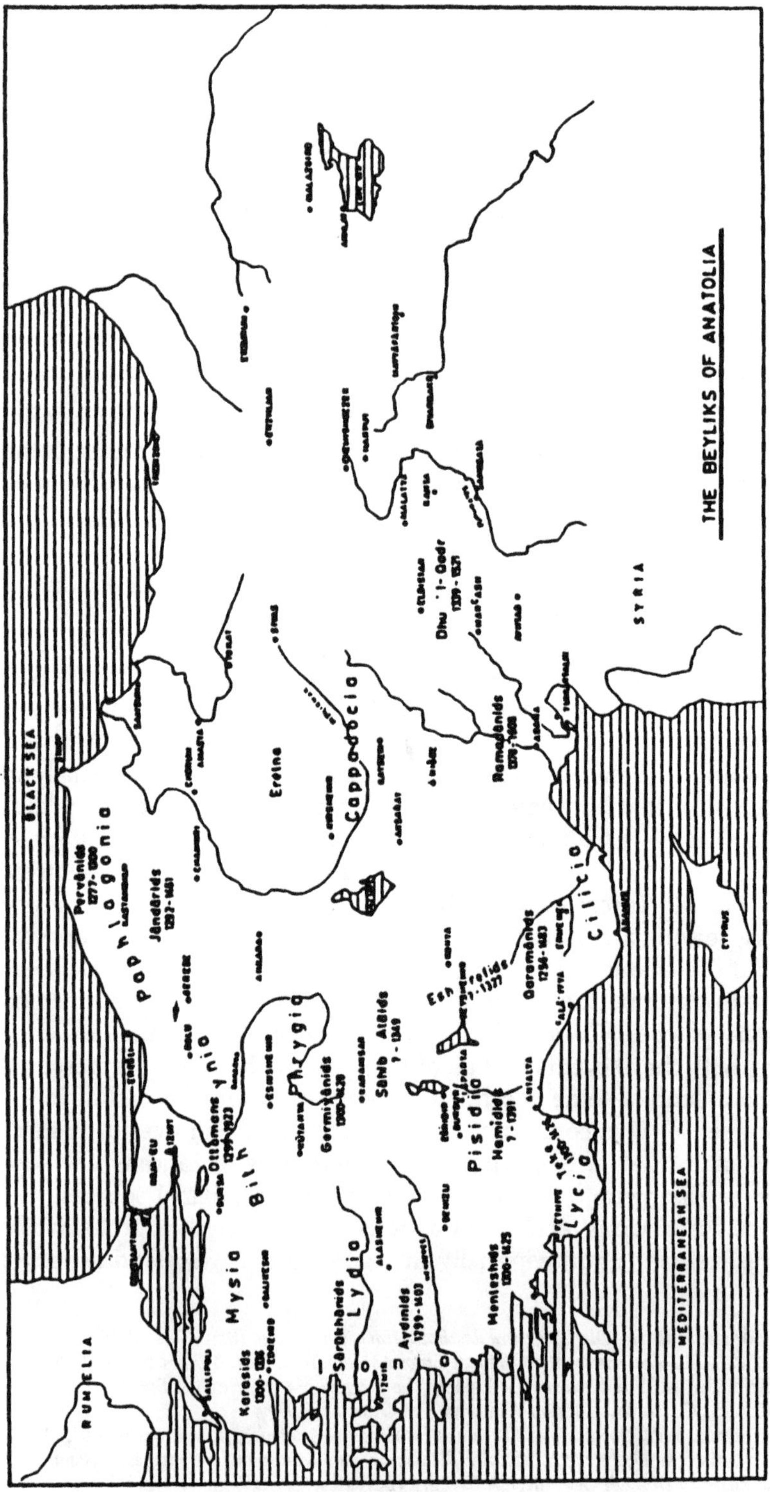

FIGURE 3.4. The Beyliks of Anatolia and dates of their establishment and disappearance, from: Köprülü, M. Fuad, trans. G. Leiser, *The Origins of the Ottoman Empire* (Albany, NY, 1992 [orig. 1935]), p. 39.

the territory and the composition of the border population. These represented boundary zones between Arab-ruled and Byzantine territories. As the invasion of Asia Minor progressed, the process can be thought of as a gradual displacement of these old boundaries toward the west, even while the Muslim forces changed from those of the ʿAbbasid khalifate to those of the Seljuk Empire. Under these conditions it is hardly surprising that the boundary elements should preserve much of their character in the process. What is new in the case of Asia Minor is that here such boundary zones, rather than coalescing into a coherent march, increasingly came to consist of numerous dissociated elements, covering, in the course of time, a substantial part of the area of the entire country, and that this situation endured for several centuries, engulfing ever new regions in frontier conditions.[135]

Frontier Population and Boundary Zones between Seljuk and Byzantine States—Ghazi, Turcoman and Akritai

The most impressive similarity between the t̲ug̲ūr of the Arabo-Byzantine boundary in the Middle East and the Turko-Byzantine frontiers in Asia Minor is revealed in the character of the populations inhabiting the two kinds of boundary zone. Their actual composition and the

---

[135] Clearly, these boundaries arose in the course of warfare. All the evidence suggests that to a large extent the conquest of Asia Minor by the Turks was the result of a long drawn-out war of motion. In this kind of warfare the extreme mobility of the Turcoman raiders contrasted with the more laborious movements of the heavily armed Imperial troops and frequently allowed the former to raid around and behind the backs of the latter. Mention of Turcomans or Ghazi warriors and their raiding activities recurs like a perpetual refrain throughout the segment of history summarized in Table 3.1. While regular disciplined troops undoubtedly played a primary role in consolidating the actual conquests, it is attractive to surmise that to a significant extent it was the role played by the irregular forces, the ghazis and their tribal allies, that laid the groundwork for the enduring occupation of the land. Indeed, at some of the critical moments these forces acted, to say the least, independently if not in direct opposition to the central government that controlled the regular troops. To cite only two instances: In the second half of the eleventh century, both before and after Manzikert, there can be little doubt that the Seljuk rulers, Alp Arslan as well as Malikshah, would have preferred to concentrate on their campaigns or campaign plans in Egypt and Ghazna rather than becoming embroiled with the Byzantines. The extraordinary treatment accorded by sultan Alp Arslan to the captive emperor Romulus Diogenes and the generous conditions offered the Byzantines testify eloquently to this preference. It was the raiding activity of the Turcomans both before and after Manzikert that forced the hand of the Seljuk sultan in spite of his wishes and caused him to dispatch his kinsman Sulaiman with a modest force to lend some air of Seljuk interest in the resulting conquests. Again, there can be no doubt that even under the Mongol protectorate over the Seljuks of Rum after their defeat at Köse Dagh, and after the return of the Basileus to Constantinople, the Seljuks would have preferred to preserve the peaceful relations they had established with the Empire of Nicea under the Lascarid emperors. Renewed Turkish attacks spearheaded by Turcoman raiding activity were resumed after 30 years of peace on this frontier, and shortly after the defeat of the Seljuks in 1243 BC by 1300 BC had resulted in the collapse of Byzantine rule in western Asia Minor. These events laid bare the weakness of that government and rendered its attempts at restraining the Turcomans ineffective. In the overall picture of the struggles between the Byzantine Empire and their Turkish opponents it is the coexistence of irregular ghazi warriors with more disciplined professional armies that appears as a recurrent theme. Raid and counter-raid produced a special kind of landscape, the borderland zone, that appears over and over as the true home of the border warriors and that as such put its stamp upon the Turko-Byzantine boundary.

circumstances involved in shaping this society are most clearly discernible in the case of the protracted events in Asia Minor and must be considered next.

As rulers the Seljuks—both the Great Seljuks and those of Rum—had successfully assimilated their government to the urbanized and sedentarized government of the former ʿAbbasid territories. Yet, it was inevitable that large numbers of those who had come from an undisguisedly tribal and nomad background should persist in their ways. Seljuk society remained a mixture of sedentarized, urbanized subjects and of nomads every bit as dependent as their forefathers upon—and as enthusiastic for—the economic benefits and the excitement of ghazua-raids upon any suitably rich and preferably sedentary peoples they could reach.

In the new setting of the Seljuk Empire such activities were sure to be perceived of as troublesome by the rulers of the state unless they could be directed away from their own subjects, preferably towards actual or potential enemies. Under the circumstances it is hardly surprising that the Seljuk rulers encouraged their tribal nomad subjects—termed Turcomans in much of the literature[136]—to raid across the borders, and especially into the relatively rich territories of the eastern portions of the Byzantine Empire.

This movement was facilitated by the pattern encountered in the transitional Turkish empires 500 years before the time of the Seljuks where there already was a spatial separation of the sedentarized (and at times urbanized) elements at the geographic core of the state from the nomad elements relegated to, or that sought out, the frontiers.[137] In view of what has been said about the makeup of the Seljuk state, it is not strange that in much the same way the tribal nomad (and raid oriented) element of its population again should have tended to congregate at the new frontiers, giving a distinct character to an awakening frontier society, different from that of the more peaceable kind of the more secure inner regions of the realm.[138] Such warriors came to be referred to as 'uç-turks', turks

---

136 Turcomans were raiding Turks said to have appeared in the Muslim literature for the first time in al-Muqaddasi's 'Description of the Muslim Empire' (al-Muqaddasi, "ahsan al-taqâsîm fi maʿrufa 'l-aqâlim," BGA III, p. 160, referring to two frontier forts near of Isbijab in ash-shâsh as "Frontier posts (sadd) against the Türks and the Ghuzz." In relation to events in medieval Asia Minor it has come to be used to describe nomad elements retaining tribal ties and economy, including a strong liking for the pleasures and the economic advantages of raiding in the age-old tradition. (cf. Низам ул-Мулк- Циясет-намэ- переводı Б.Н.Заходера- Москва 1949), p. 109 regarding the role of Turcomans in the Seljuk state). These elements were primarily, but not exclusively, Turkish; they included among others some Kurdish groups. It is sometimes assumed that frontier warriors falling into this category, can be distinguished from, though at times associated with, ghazi, warriors (cf. Cahen, C., trans. J. Jones-Williams, *Pre-Ottoman Turkey* [New York, NY, 1968], p. 58 comparing Turcomans in the army with Turcomans 'riding as ghazi')—supposed to have been driven by religious motives—a view that I, in accord with Lindner (Lindner, R.P., *Nomads and Ottomans in Medieval Anatolia* (Bloomington, Ind., 1983) find implausible (see below for discussion of this point).

137 McGovern, W.M., *The Early Empires of Central Asia* (Chapel Hill, 1939).

138 Wittek, P., *The Rise of the Ottoman Empire* (New York, NY, 1971) (original 1938) and Wittek, P., *Das Fürstentum Mentesche* (Istanbul, 1934).

of the frontiers (the Turkish 'uç' means either 'frontier' or 'the point of a weapon' and thus is closely analogous to the etymology of the Arabic 'thughûr', cf. footnote 18).[139] These made up the core of the border population but were joined by other warlike elements, including displaced Armenians and Slavs as well as Islamized members of the pre-conquest Byzantine provincial society, all combining to form what Wittek called the "mixed border population." Because the Turks swept over ever larger parts of the peninsula, the frontier between Byzantine and Turk became more complex and disjointed in the course of the ensuing wars, and uç-Turks were introduced into additional partially devastated districts from which by no means all the Greek inhabitants had fled,[140] creating further regions that to a significant degree acquired the characteristics of a Greco-Turkic frontier society (cf. Table 3.2 that calls attention to the similarity in the general makeup of the border population in Anatolia and in the Syrian and Jazirian t̲ugūr).

Adding weight to the resulting movement was that by this time many of the Turkish tribes had been Islamicized for several decades, and Islamicized for the most part by somewhat heterodox but all the more ardent dervish preachers. Among the duties that these promulgated with particular vigor was that of pursuing the Holy War against the Unbeliever, and especially the unreformed Christian. Men who took upon themselves this obligation were popularly referred to as ghāzī—perhaps an unintentional indication that what was aimed at was the 'ghazu' the term in its original meaning as used to this day among the Bedouin of Arabia for the cattle and slave raid in the ancient tradition. Thus, for these unrecondite marauders the economic attractions of raiding into Byzantine territory were reinforced by the religious motif that made folk heros out of what might otherwise have been no more than successful invaders.[141] The poems singing of the exploits of Dede Qorqut,[142] of the Melik Danishmend[143] and of Sayyid Battal[144] bear witness to this phenomenon. Historians have debated the relative weight given among these ghazis to economic motivation and to the primarily religious motivation of devout Muslim warriors engaging in Holy War against infidel Greeks in accordance with Qur'anic mandate. Some have focused their attention upon the self-description of these warriors as 'ghazis' to infer a dominant religious motive[76] while others have noted that these 'ghazis' did not by any means restrict their raiding and war-making to infidel opponents or to heretics, but gleefully and in more than one location also attacked orthodox believers.[145] It seems to me that the argument is somewhat

---

[139] Köprülü, M. Fuad, trans. G. Leiser, *The Origins of the Ottoman Empire*, 78; Barthold, W., *Turkestan down to the Mongol Invasion*, 2nd edition (London, 1958), 61.

[140] Vryonis, *The Decline of Medieval Hellenism in Asia Minor and the Process of Islamization from the Eleventh through the Fifteenth Century* (Berkeley, CA, 1971), p. 25.

[141] Wittek, P., *The Rise of the Ottoman Empire* (New York, NY, 1971) (original 1938).

[142] Rossi, E., trans., *Il Kitab-i Dede Qorqut* (Città del Vaticano, 1952).

[143] Melikoff, P., trans., *La geste de Melik* (Danishmend, Paris, 1960).

[144] Ethé, H., trans., *Die Fahrten des Sayyid Battal* (Leipzig, 1871).

[145] Lindner, R.P., *Nomads and Ottomans in Medieval Anatolia*, 78.

TABLE 3.2. Composition of the Mixed Border Population

In al-Andalus	In Syrian and Jazirian ṯuġūr	In Anatolian border zones
Berbers (from sedentary tribes) [In middle and lower ṯuġūr]	Arab tribesmen (Qaisites)	Turkish tribesmen (uç turcoman)
Arabs [in upper ṯuġūr]	Iranian tribesmen	(Arab tribesmen)
Celtiberians and Visigoths [largely displaced]	Slavs	(Slavs)
	Gypsies (Zott, Sayābigā) Jarājima	Armenians Islamized Greeks
	Original Population (Armenians, Syrians)	
[Bosch Vilá-Albarracin Musulman]	[Wellhausen-Das Arabische Reich] [Canard-Djarādjima]	[Wittek-Das Königreich Mentesche]

futile. Clearly, the logics of the case render this not an 'either/or' but rather an 'and' kind of situation.

The numbers of warriors of this kind and of associated nomadic groups converging upon Asia Minor were swelled, especially during the thirteenth century, by nomads displaced from their pasture lands by the advances of the Mongols across Khwarezm and much of Persia.

The existence of such a warlike border society did not remain without influence upon the conduct of the hostilities between Byzantines and their Muslim opponents. Curbing the movement of these frontier warriors—and especially adjusting the timing and the intensity of their raiding activities—to conform to some sophisticated political motives could not be easy for any central government. Indeed, throughout the 300 year-long campaigns that eventually made Hellenistic Asia Minor over into Turkey one finds that events are apt to be driven by two distinct wills, not infrequently in conflict (cf. note 129): On one side is a central government with aspirations of restoring the Islāmic Empire as it had been during the heyday of the ʿAbbasids by the carefully timed and directed use of organized troops made up increasingly of slave levies as the tribal element was thinned out. On the other hand we find the unruly Turcoman and ghazi forces, more concerned with booty, pasture, and the Holy War than with the strengthening of a state that they saw as little more than a relentless collector of taxes.[146,147] Ghazi raids thrusting beyond or around the advances of the regular armies are, in consequence, a frequent feature of these wars and could not fail to have a profound influence upon the configuration of the actual boundary.

---

146 Cf. e.g., Cahen, C., trans. J. Jones-Williams, *Pre-Ottoman Turkey*, 103; and Köprülü, M. Fuad, trans. G. Leiser, *The Origins of the Ottoman Empire*, 78.

147 Cahen, C., trans. J. Jones-Williams, *Pre-Ottoman Turkey*, 88; and Pertusi, A., "Tra storia e leggenda: Akritai e ghazi sulla frontiera orientale di Bisanzo" in: *Rapports du XIV Congrès International des Études Bizantines, IIe thème: Frontières et Régions Frontières du VIIe au XIIe siècle (les Frontières Asiatiques)* (Bucarest, 1971), 68.

A final factor influencing the character of the society emerging in the border districts was the situation on the Byzantine side of the border. This was somewhat similar to that on the Turkish side but, if anything, more complex. Here, too, one finds border warriors dedicated, like the ghazis, to unremitting frontier war of raid and—especially, as it turned out—defense against raids. By choice, Byzantine frontiers were laid wherever possible in regions where natural defenses made defense easy, especially mountains and mountain passes. From the Greek term for such passes these warriors came to be known as Akritai (at a later stage some of the frontier fighters were known as 'apelatoi', a name with somewhat derogatory implications and not entirely clear meaning, while the term 'Akritas' came to be restricted to the leaders of such frontier forces).[148] Unlike the ghazi one does not encounter mention in the literature that these Greek frontier warriors engaged in extensive raiding—their role in the centuries here under consideration seems to have been in large measure defensive. One may wonder to what extent this difference arose from the historical situation in which they were cast, and to what extent it may reflect that the Akritai arose in a sedentary rather than a predominantly nomad society. Like the ghazi they formed a population the composition of which was distinct from that of the peaceful hinterland. Among other warlike elements they, too, included not a few Turks, largely, it seems, brought in from the north, with Bulghar and Slavic elements.[149] Thus, the march population on the Byzantine side was not altogether different from that on the Muslim side. However, in contrast to the ghazis, these Byzantine frontier warriors counted on substantial direct support from the state, in terms not only of remission of taxes and assignment of lands—these applied as well to the uç-Turks—but also in terms of direct subventions. When these sources of support were tampered with, as they were under the Paleologi, Byzantine frontier warriors were prone to desert to the enemy and the subsequent collapse of the defenses in that case testifies to the importance of the Akritai as guardian of the borders.[150]

The border populations on the two sides of the boundary thus shared

---

148 Roux, J.-P., "Le cheval et le chameau en Asie Centrale," *Central Asiatic Journal* 5 (1959): 35–76, p. 76; Ahrweiler, H., "La Frontière et les Frontières de Byzance en Orient" in: *Rapports du XIV Congrès International des Études Bizantines, IIe thème, Frontières et Régions Frontières du VIIe au XIIe siècle (les Frontières Asiatiques)* (Bucarest, 1971), p. 14; Pertusi, a. "Tra storia e leggenda: Akritai e ghazi sulla frontiera orientale di Bisanzo" in: *Rapports du XIV Congrès International des Études Bizantines, IIe thème, Frontières et Régions Frontières du VIIe au XIIe siècle (les Frontières Asiatiques)* (Bucarest, 1971), p. 37; Lindner, R.P., *Nomads and Ottomans in Medieval Anatolia*, 12.

149 Vasiliev, A.A., *History of the Byzantine Empire*, vol. 1 (Madison, Wisc., 1964), 576 ff.; Honigmann, E., *Die Ostgrenze des Byzantinischen Reiches* (Bruxelles, 1935), 40.

150 Lindner, R.P., *Nomads and Ottomans in Medieval Anatolia*, 17, 38–40; Pertusi, a., "Tra storia e leggenda: Akritai e ghazi sulla frontiera orientale di Bisanzo" in: *Rapports du XIV Congrès International des Études Bizantines, IIe thème, Frontières et Régions Frontières du VIIe au XIIe siècle* (Bucarest, 1971), p. 37; Köprülü, M. Fuad, trans. G. Leiser, *The Origins of the Ottoman Empire*, 80 and note that Lindner, p. 17ff. also comments on the importance of encroachment of big land owners on landholdings of small farmers at the border in contributing to their loss of interest in frontier defense.

many basic attitudes and experiences. Similar occupations added weight to the groups on either side of an ill-defined frontier's perception that they had more than a little in common—in spite of the alleged profound differences created by adherence to different religions, and at times loudly proclaimed themselves 'warriors of the(ir respective) faith(s).' Intermarriage provided a subject for some of the most famous romances on both sides of the frontier.[151] Travelers' reports and the romances and epics of the period confirm that out of them arose a mixed border society, more or less homogeneous within itself but profoundly different from the population of the undisturbed hinterland on either side. In the course of time it comprised a mixture of Turkish frontier fighters, Byzantine frontier fighters (Akritai and Apelatoi) including not a few Turks and Slavs, and, as the frontier conditions endured, a substantial proportion of the old residents of the conquered territories.[152] To the extent that these borderlands represented a region largely indifferent to government control, they were also places of refuge for martial elements fallen out of favor with the central government.[153]

Thus, this border population constituted a distinct element in the Seljuk state and its successors. Distinct in many ways from the urbanized and sedentarized elements of the core areas, it also was in many ways unlike the nomadic and tribal elements subsisting at a distance from the frontier. Unlike what seems to have been true in the Near East where the ṯugūr accounted for a small fraction only of both space and population, the history of Asia Minor in the first three centuries of the present millennium caused these frontier zones to engulf a substantial part of the peninsula and hence to have a major effect on the characteristics of the emerging society of the newly formed Ottoman Turkey. In this sense it seems clear that the boundary zones that developed in the course of the Turkish conquest of Asia Minor did indeed perform at least one key frontier function in the sense of Turner and his critics.[154]

The Turks' conquest of Asia Minor is part of their advance toward the West—one arm of a movement of these central Asiatic peoples away from a region that was becoming both more crowded and climatically more inhospitable to the activities of nomadic pastoralists.[155] In the thirteenth century the impetus of this movement was increased under the impact of

---

151 Cf. e.g., Digenis Akritas, *The two-blood Border Lord*, D.B. Hull trans. (Akron, Ohio, 1972).

152 Pertusi, a., "Tra storia e leggenda: Akritai e ghazi sulla frontiera orientale di Bisanzo" in: *Rapports du XIV Congrès International des Études Bizantines, IIe thème, Frontières et Régions Frontières du VIIe au XIIe siècle (les Frontières Asiatiques)* (Bucarest, 1971), p. 38; and Canard, M., *Les rélations politiques et siciales entre Byzance et les Arabes* (Dumbarton Oaks Papers 18, 1964), p. 45; and note that Cahen, C., trans. J. Jones-Williams, *Pre-Ottoman Turkey*, 63, presents evidence for not infrequent fraternization between border warriors from the two sides fraternizing.

153 Cf. e.g., Wittek, P., *Das Fürstentum Mentesche*, 6.

154 Turner, F.J., *The Frontier in American History* (New York, NY, 1920); and Walsh, M., *The American Frontier Revisited* (Atlantic Highlands, NJ, 1967); also cf. Discussion in Section 3 below.

155 Climate in central Asia in twelfth to fourteenth century.

the Mongol conquests.[156] The unique development of the frontiers we have seen in Asia Minor in the long course of the conflict between Byzantium and the Turks, however, remains unexplained unless one takes into account the presence of the frontier warriors at the borders between the two. In particular the ghazi on the Turkish side represent warriors wholly dedicated to aggressive frontier war, possessed of extraordinary mobility, retaining links with the nomadic society from which a great part of them sprang, and are responsible for the extraordinary resilience of the "mixed frontier population" in shifting from warrior to pastoral means of gaining a livelihood. The historical accounts show them everywhere associated with the Turko-Byzantine boundary, and with the recurrent formation of a boundary zone consisting of no-man's land that yet was not void of inhabitants. Comparison with their counterparts on the Byzantine side has revealed the many points of similarity between the two bodies of frontier warriors, and their prolonged association renders plausible their melding to form a mixed frontier society that provided a boundary zone population distinct in many ways from that of the peaceful hinterland—a society inclined to assimilate rather than to exclude other population elements.[157] Only such a society existing over centuries under the shifting conditions of the struggle between Byzantium and the Turkish invaders can account for the events that converted conquered hellenized Asia Minor into Ottoman Turkey.

We have here the conditions that gave rise to the boundary zones that were so prominent in Asia Minor. As was shown in the first section of this essay, similar structures were shown to be present in two other theaters that saw the development of boundary zones in place of boundary lines between Muslim and Infidel societies: the ṯugūr at the northern extremity of the Arabo-Islāmic Empire, and those that intervened between largely Berberized forces in the Iberian Peninsula and the Christian kingdoms that persisted in the northern part of that peninsula. The common denominator among these events is the association of the zone type of external boundary with Muslim nomads (cf. Table 3.2). At least three different nomad populations were involved in these events: Turkish ghazis and Turcoman tribesmen, Arab Bedouin, and Berbers; thus, within the narrow limits of the available evidence the tribal identity of these nomads would appear to have been of secondary importance. In each case, too, the nomad population involved was associated with other elements that formed part of a fully organized state, soldiers as well as administrators. In the case of the Turks considered in the preceding

---

[156] Kwanten, L., *Imperial Nomads.*

[157] З.В. Удалцова, А.П. Каждан, Р.М.,Бортикиян- Социалная структура восточных границ византииской Империй- in: *Rapports du XIV Congrès International des Études Bizantines, IIe thème, Frontières et Régions Frontières du VIIe au XIIe siècle (les Frontières Asiatiques)* (Bucarest, 1971), pp. 21, 26; Ahrweiler, H., *La Frontière et les Frontières de Byzance en Orient* in: *Rapports du XIV Congrès International des Études Bizantines, IIe thème, Frontières et Régions Frontières du VIIe au XIIe siècle (les Frontières Asiatiques)* (Bucarest, 1971), p. 16.

pages these elements were made up of the several states directly involved – the Great Seljuks, the Seljuks of Rum, the Ottomans, the ghazi beyliks (though the latter proved unstable and do not seem to have contributed to any great degree to the eventual course of affairs). In the case of the Arabs of the Futuh, the contrast between Bedouin warrior nomads and the denizens of the cities was unmistakable from the time of the Prophet Muhammad on and persisted into the time of the ʿAbassids when the regular army had come to be increasingly staffed by slave soldiers.[158] In the case of the conquests on the Iberian Peninsula the burden of the fighting was carried largely by Berber troops while the government of the Emirate of al-Andalus was largely dominated by the more sophisticated Arabs who saw to it that the frontier regions, especially those in the more inhospitable mountain regions would become the home of the former soldiers.[159]

It is tempting to see in this common pattern a special version of the antinomy between 'the desert and the sown' perceived by Ibn Khaldun as the main driving force of history in North Africa.[160]

Appendix

The Historical Sequence of the Events Leading to the Conversion of Byzantine Asia Minor to Ottoman Turkey

Predecessors of the Turkish tribes that eventually impinged upon the Byzantine Empire are recognizable at least as far back as the second century before the present era: the Hsiung-Nu that appear in Han Chinese historiography were horse nomads probably akin to the later Turks, occupied the eastern portions of the Central Asiatic steppe region, northwest of the borders of the Han Empire (Fig. 1). They showed considerable organizational and military aptitude as mounted archers, and may well have been the ancestors of the Huns that overran much of Europe in the first century of our era. The literature suggests that they gave little weight to the individual ownership of land and to frontiers.[161] Yet, they had a strong sense of the importance of holding on to tribal lands as witness the statement of the Hsiung Nu ruler Mao Tun (ca. -190 A.D.): "Land is the basis of a state; disintegration of a tribe is inevitable when its land is lost."[162] Turks appear first under that name as iron workers to the Yuan Yuan in the sixth century. From the earliest mention of them on they appear as a people that was not purely nomadic; pastoral nomads among them coexisted with farmers and blacksmiths[163] – a pattern that in later times allowed the coexistence of sedentary and nomadic turkish elements within the confines of the highly urbanized Seljuk state.

---

158 Bedouin vs. urban, Hodgson, *Venture of Islam*.

159 Bosh Vila, J., *Albarracin Musulman- El reino de taifas de los Beni Razín, hasta la constitución del señorío Cristiano* (Teruel, 1959), 65, 66; Fletcher, R., *Moorish Spain* (New York, NY, 1992) 19–20.

160 Ibn Khaldun, *The Muqaddimah*, F. Rosenthal trans. (New York, NY, 1958).

161 Cahen, C., trans. J. Jones-Williams, *Pre-Ottoman Turkey*, 3.

162 Watson, B., *Records of the Great Historian of China* (New York, 1961), p. 2:162; also Kwanten, L., *Imperial Nomads* (Philadelphia, PA, 1979), p. 43.

163 Kwanten, L., *Imperial Nomads*, 32 ff.

A Turkic empire arose in the steppes of eastern Central Asia by the fifth century but broke up sometime before the end of the eighth under attacks from Chinese and Tibetan forces[164] to give way to the formation of a number of successor states such as the Uighur, the Qaraqanid (according to Cahen the first of the truly Turkish states–in contrast to others such as the Ghaznavid state, that were in fact Islamic states ruled by Turkish ghulam [ex-slave soldier] princes[165]), Qarluq, and, a bit later, the Khwarezmian and Seljuk empires.[166] All of these, it is reported, were sedentarized, separated from one another by wide frontier zones inhabited by Turkic nomad tribes. As will be seen presently, this core-and-frontier-zone pattern, too, was carried by the Turks into their occupation of pre-Ottoman Asia Minor.

At the beginning of the tenth century the region south of the Caspian and Aral Seas immediately east of the Persian desert (the Khorasan) and extending into the southern reaches of the Land beyond the River (Oxus)–Mā wara' n-nāhr or Transoxania–had fallen to Arabo-Iranian advances and then, under two of the Khalif's governors, had become largely independent of Baghdad to form the Samānid and Ghaznavid states. For a time, the Samānid state constituted the border between Islamicized lands and at best very incompletely Islamicized Turkic Qaraqanids. Beyond the northern border of the Samānid state, between the Caspian and the Aral Sea and for some distance to the east of the regions dominated by the Qaraqanids were the lands of the Oghuz tribes to whom the Seljuks trace their origin[167] (cf. Fig. 2a).

In a kaleidoscopic series of changes the next sixty years saw the disintegration of the Samānid state and its conquest by the Ghaznavids by 1030 AD, the expansion of the Oghuzz holdings to occupy most of the Khorasan by 1050, and the projection of Seljuk power through central Persia into Baghdad, overthrowing the Buyid usurpers of the 'Abbasid power[168] and forming a firm alliance with the Khalif.

The eleventh century[169] witnessed the entry of the Seljuks into Baghdad and the recognition of their chief as the Sultan by the Khalif. Sultan Toghrul as well as his successor Alp Arslan adopted as their grand strategy the concept of a restored Sunni orthodox Islāmic Empire including Egypt as well as the marches of India; the conquests this implied required that the Seljuks should keep their western flank safe by ensuring peaceful relations with their Byzantine neighbors. By contrast, autonomous nomadic groups of Islamized Turcomans entering the region saw a rich opportunity for plunder in the wealthy western provinces of Byzantium and began a series of raids beyond the frontiers of the Seljuk territories from about 1020 AD on, even while the Seljuk armies studiously avoided any confrontations with the Greek Empire. The battle of Manzikert changed that situation insofar as here Alp Arslan effectively destroyed the ability of Byzantium to defend its eastern frontier. This in turn allowed what had been a pattern of isolated Turcoman raids to swell to a flood that presently engulfed all of Asia Minor from the Armenian marches to the Aegean Sea. In this advance Seljuk

---

164 Ibid., 27–48.

165 Cahen, C., trans. J. Jones-Williams, *Pre-Ottoman Turkey*, 10–11.

166 Kwanten, L., *Imperial Nomads*, 49ff.

167 Houtsma, M.Th., "Die Ghuzenstämme," *Wiener Zschr. f/d/ Kunde des Morgenlandes* 2 (1888): 219–233.

168 Hourani, A., *A History of the Arab Peoples*, 296.

169 For references upon which this and the succeeding paragraphs of the Appendix are based see text of the section above.

troops and Seljuk leadership became involved only haltingly, entering the fray only after the floodgates of what amounted to a Turkish mass migration had opened. By the end of the century all of Asia Minor from the Armenian and Georgian marches to the shores of the Aegean Sea was in Seljuk hands.

Turcoman raiders now no longer invariably returned with their booty to wherever they had started from but in many cases came to stay among the earlier inhabitants in what had been Byzantine lands. Some of these newly resident Turcomans now remained as apparently peaceful transhumant herdsmen yet retained their potentially aggressive inclinations, while others showed themselves undisguisedly as frontier warriors entirely dependent for their livelihood upon booty and the sale of prisoners in eastern slave markets. Contacts with the residual Byzantine population were inevitable and by no means always hostile, and even at this early time would seem to have included some cross marriages. The entire process resulted in the formation of a mixed border society much like that familiar from the Syrian and Mesopotamian ṯuġūr, a society that would presently become characteristic of much of Asia Minor. This stage also saw the establishment of the state of the Seljuks of Rum, its capital first in Nicea and later in Konia, as an entity increasingly independent of the Near Eastern Great Seljuks though inclined to copy their aspiration to be recognized as a bona fide Islamic state. In contrast to this, Turcoman warriors carved out for themselves what has been called a 'ghazi state', identified with the Turcoman ghazi warrior chief Danishmend. This entity came into being not long after the battle of Manzikert and for about a century dominated the northern central parts of Anatolia.

Byzantium had seen a great deal of internal unrest during the century. This had weakened its military stance as well as it border defenses and contributed greatly to the defeat at Manzikert. Near the end of the eleventh century, however, the passage of the army of the First Crusade had brought it military aid that had allowed it to recoup some of its defensive strength and to recover much of western Asia Minor and of the southern coastal districts, forcing the Turkish elements back onto the Anatolian Plateau. The advance of the Byzantines came to an end with their crushing defeat at the hands of the Seljuks at Myriokephalon, a defeat again in part attributable to the harassing activities of autonomous Turcoman raiders. During this period the Danishmend state broke up in the course of internal quarrels, leaving the Seljuks as the dominating force in Turkish Asia Minor.

By the end of the twelfth century they had recovered the territory lost to the Byzantine counterattack and once again were masters of all of Asia Minor. The thirteenth century opened with the conquest of Constantinople by the armies of the Fourth Crusade and the consequent displacement of the Byzantine Basileus from the European continent to exile in Nicea, resulting in the formation of the Nicean Empire out of the remaining Byzantine holdings in Asia Minor under the government of the capable Lascarids. The attention of the Empire now came to be concentrated on Asia Minor, strengthening its military position there to the point where western Asia Minor was once more recovered from the Turks, so that the Byzantine-Turkish frontier was pushed eastward well onto the Anatolian plateau. The military strengthening of the Byzantines was by force recognized by the Turks and provided the basis for nearly a half century of peaceful and even friendly relations between Seljuks and Lascarids, a period marked by thirty years' suspension of Turcoman raiding into the Empire.

The next stage was predicted beginning early in the thirteenth century by the appearance in eastern Asia Minor of numerous Central Asian Turks displaced as a result of Mongol advances. There is evidence of unrest among Turcoman elements within the confines of the Seljuk state in Asia Minor: the revolt associated with the name of Baba Ishaq was at base a religious disturbance but assumed threatening proportions because it was taken up by disaffected elements on the frontiers. On the Turkish side this situation was rendered more threatening when at Köse Dagh Seljuk forces suffered a disastrous defeat at the hands of a relatively small detachment of Mongol troops, and when, to the displeasure of its ghazi warriors, the Seljuk government showed itself increasingly subservient to Mongol dictates in the sequel. By the end of the century, the Seljuks of Rum, increasingly deprived of the support of the warrior elements that had been the backbone of its strength, faded into insignificance. Simultaneously, the peace with the Byzantines was increasingly compromised by Turcoman ghazi raiding activities across the western frontier when these tribes no longer recognized any check on their activities by the fading Seljuk government. Indeed, by the year 1300 AD the Seljuk state had in effect vanished.

The final stage in the process of Turkification of Asia Minor had been initiated around the middle of the thirteenth century by the formation of a whole series of Ghazi beyliks–states dominated by warlike elements of the type spawned on the frontiers–Germian, Mentesche, Karaman, Osmanli, numerous and often in conflict with one another at their several frontiers. Simultaneously there emerged a number of essentially pirate beyliks along the western and southern coasts of Asia Minor–Sarukhan, Aydin, Karasi, Tekke, Sinope. It is interesting to speculate that these states may have transferred the concept of a no-man's land along the terrestrial borders to the seas adjacent to the peninsula of Asia Minor.

In any event, these developments were ominous from the point of view of the Byzantine holdings in Asia Minor, compromised once more when in 1261 the Latin rulers were expelled from Constantinople and the seat of the Empire returned from Nicea in Asia Minor to Constantinople on the European shore of the Hellespont. With this move, the focus of interest of the Empire shifted back to its European domain, accompanied by relative neglect of its affairs in Asia Minor. Simultaneously, the Lascarids were replaced by the Paleologue dynasty that, in confronting its increasing fiscal difficulties, chose to do so by infringing on the old established privileges of its border troops in Asia Minor–forfeiting what loyalty to the state these border warriors had retained–as well as disestablishing the powerful Byzantine war fleet in 1284 AD. The result was that the territory gained by the Lascarids in the mid-thirteenth century was lost: by the end of that century all of Asia Minor once more came into Turkish hands and for the most part has remained there since.

The fourteenth century is marked by the rapid progress of the Ottoman state as the dominant factor in Asia Minor at the expense of the smaller beyliks that had arisen in the second half of the thirteenth century. The check of Ottoman development at the hands of Timur-i Lang in the battle of Ankara in 1402 AD, the subsequent development of Ottoman domination in eastern Europe, and the fall of Constantinople to Sultan Mehmed II, all fall outside the period of concern in the present context. From the middle of the thirteenth century on military activity in the region was increasingly carried out by organized armies under close control by the rulers of the several states, and with this development the kind of border no-man's land that concerns us receded into insignificance.

SECTION 4

Summary and Conclusions

We have now concluded the presentation of what seemed to us the essential factual material bearing on boundary concepts in the medieval Islamic world. It will be useful at this point to recapitulate briefly the course of the inquiry to this point:

> The observation giving rise to this study was that indications of political boundaries are altogether absent from the greatest of the Muslim geography treatises, the twelfth century "Book of Roger" of the geographer al-Idrisi working at the court of the Norman ruler of Sicily. It was demonstrated that in fact medieval Arabo-Islamic geographers, from the earliest scholars working at the beginning of the ninth century right through to the fourteenth century days of Ibn Khaldun, if they admitted the existence of political boundaries at all, did not conceive of the margins of adjoining individual states as sharp borderlines. Regardless of whether they addressed boundaries formed by states falling within Dar al-Islam or between Dar al-Islam as a whole and states of Unbelievers, geographers described all such borders in terms implying boundary zones of significant depth surrounding a core area for any given political entity within which its capital was located. Transition zones associated with external frontiers were shown to be occupied by a mixed border population differing in its composition from that of the core areas of these states. A hypothesis was formulated to describe the conception of the territory of a state implied by these characteristics.
>
> Along with this perception of boundaries as transition zones, the concept of 'area' as a descriptor of geographic facts was shown to be absent from the medieval Muslim literature dealing with geographical concepts.
>
> The transition zone concept of political boundaries was not confined to the scholars but rather corresponded to the experience of the people of the time as reflected in travel accounts that imply that there was nothing to inform a traveler that he was approaching or crossing a political boundary; customs and document control in general were experienced in towns, by no means always near any frontier.
>
> Boundaries involving Muslim territory on one side and 'unbeliever' territory on the other were shown to have been characterized by the development of a system of defense in depth, consisting of primary frontier zones, ṯuġūr, and awāṣīm. The ṯuġūr were shown to have encompassed fortress towns and lesser fortresses in a wider defense zone under military administration, and to have been occupied by a distinct boundary population, differing from both the regular armies and the rural as well as urban population of the Muslim-states involved. The origins of the terms were traced and it was shown that reference to such structures is widespread in the geographical literature of the time, but that in the works of any given author the concept seems to have been given but slight emphasis.

All of these observations were based on data from Arabo-Iranian societies. For comparison, a study was reported concerning the displacement of antique hellenistic Byzantine communities in Asia Minor by Seljuk and Ottoman Turkish ones during the conquest of Byzantine Asia Minor by the Seljuks and their successors during the period from the eleventh to the fourteenth century. Development of boundary zones even more extensive than in the Near East or the Iberian Peninsula was encountered in this case, and was shown to have been associated with the formation of a distinct "mixed border population" made up of border fighters from both sides together with political or religious refugees and a remnant of the original inhabitants. In the course of the protracted warfare associated with these events the actual boundary swept over a large part of the Anatolian peninsula, and thus by the time of the Ottoman predominance in the peninsula a considerable fraction of the population remaining in the region had been subjected to border conditions and to the processes of assimilation to which they gave rise.

Closer examination of the actual progression of events showed that the fighting involved, in addition to the organized armies of essentially sedentary societies, irregular frontier warriors – ghazis on the Muslim side – still closely linked to a nomadic way of life and more often than not fighting as autonomous units in raids uncorrelated with the campaigns of the Turkish princes ruling the states or beyliks involved.

In retrospect, these characteristics of the conquest of Asia Minor by the Turks were seen to find close parallels in earlier Muslim conquests, dominated by Bedouin Arabs in the Middle East and by Berbers and Arabs on the Iberian Peninsula, and leading to the formation of ṯugūr and awāṣīm in those settings. Thus, the available data suggest that zone boundaries surrounding the core of a given state may be a phenomenon common to Muslim conquest societies.

It was shown finally that the concept of zone frontiers reflects basic religious as well as administrative and ethnic tenets of the culture of the medieval Muslim world, summarized in Table 4.1.

It is now possible to recast these data to examine the principal questions we have answered as well as those that remain to be answered and that may call for additional factual data.

The inquiry confirms the division of boundaries in the minds of the Muslim scholars into two types: Internal (between two Muslim states) and External (between a Muslim and a non-Muslim state) boundaries.

Examination of the dynastic history of the Islamic Empire reveals a progression from a single unitary Dār al-Islām to a system of at least 15 states, confirming the existence of numerous Internal boundaries within the realm of Islām from the ninth century on despite the original religious emphasis on a single Umma.

The geographers' concept of zone type boundaries at these interfaces was shown to correspond to the experiences of travelers. This concept and the insignificant importance attached to political boundaries within Dār al-Islām it implies would seem to have been of fundamental importance to the preservation of what may be called the medieval Islamic "common trade zone."[170]

---

[170] Richards, D.S., ed., *Islam and the Trade of Asia*, Oxford 1970, especially articles by B. Spuler and A.L. Udovitch.

TABLE 4.1. Factors and Attitudes Tending to Favor Vagueness of Geographical Boundaries in Medieval Islamic Society

Qur'ān and Hadīth
Command of brotherhood of all members of 'Umma
Mandate of permanent jihād against unbelievers
Concept that all land belongs to Allah
Geographers' and Administrators' Attitudes
Non-use of Area concept
Complexity of land tax structure
Concept of the state as a sum of its cities
Structure of society
Persistence of Bedouin concepts of rights flowing from land ownership
Predominance of cities (and city/kura complexes) in political and commercial life
Coexistence of sedentary and nomad elements in the population
Individuals
Absence of concept of citizenship
Acquired as well as category-determined loyalties to individuals only—not corporate entities

This material confirms the impression that these scholars' writings conformed closely to popularly held concepts of the characteristics of medieval Muslim geography. In addition, we made the significant point that geographers do not seem to have made any use of the concept of area in their writings. Since that concept was thoroughly familiar to early Arabo-Islamic mathematicians, this attitude would seem to represent another example of poor communication between Muslim specialists in the theoretical and applied sciences (elsewhere we have called attention to a similar disparity between the understanding of Muslim geographers and, in that case, navigators with regard to determination and significance of latitude south of the equator).[171]

External frontiers of the type designated in the Arabo-Islamic literature ṯugūr were shown to develop at all interfaces between a Muslim and a non-Muslim dominated country and only there. They have been characterized as zone type boundaries, and their geographic distribution as well as the distribution of fortress towns and of lesser fortresses within them have been described.

With these data we concluded that, in accordance with Ibn Khaldun's dictum, medieval Muslim states were indeed conceived of as being surrounded on all sides by boundary zones and hence lacked the sharply defined territory that would require border lines. Clearly, one could conclude that such states cannot have been conceived of as territorial states by the people of the time.

---

[171] Brauer, R.W., "The Dynamics of Change in the Magnitude of Geographical Coordinates in Three Civilizations," *American Neptune* 53 [4]: (1993).

TABLE 4.2. Comparison of Boundary Characteristics in Asia Minor and Near East

Subject	Arab conquests in Near East	Turkification of Asia Minor
	The warfare	
time course of warfare	Quick advance then relatively stable frontier	sustained struggle, frontier shifting back and forth
non-Muslim opponent	Byzantine, Sassanid Empires	Byzantine Empire, crusaders
nature of invading forces	Arab tribesmen under (more or less unified) command	Seljuk professional army plus turcoman and ghazi warriors operating independently
tribal structure	acephalous, segmental	conical, chief-oriented
numbers of conquerors	small initially, never large	modest initially, growing continuously
	The results	
progress of islamization in zone	rapid, but initially limited	gradual, partly reflecting exodus of Christians
character of boundary zone	continuous strip	broken up and mosaic
appearance of landscape	no-man's land	no-man's land
cities and fortifications	present in thughur, defensive system	inconsistent
population of opposing side of border	scarce; deliberately depopulated	Akritai and associated border fighters
blending of opposing border populations	limited information, some border elements crossed back and forth	literature suggests considerable intercourse

This configuration of the boundaries was shown to follow in large measure from certain religious mandates. It was suggested that these reflect the essentially transcendental character of the Islamic state. Other evidence, for example, the concept that such states reserved to themselves a monopoly (or a near monopoly) of the use of force, modifies this view and leads to the perception that in the medieval Muslim world the idea of the state was a hybrid one in the sense of Watt.[172]

Comparison of events leading to the formation of boundary zones in connection with the Arab conquests of the seventh and eighth century and the Seljuk conquests in Asia Minor in the tenth to fourteenth showed (Table 4.2) that, while boundary zones were formed in both cases, the events leading to their formation as well as the configuration of the structures actually developed showed certain differences as well as similarities and the significance of these requires further analysis. On

[172] Watt, W.M., *Islam and the Integration of Society* (Edinburgh, 1960), c.V.

the one hand the differences may reflect the different nature of the warfare giving rise to the boundaries in the two situations – the penetrating initial conquests of the Arabs as compared to the seesaw character of the Turko-Byzantine conflict. On the other hand, it may be worthwhile to consider that the character of the conquests reflected underlying differences in the social structure of the tribal societies from which the two conquering forces were ultimately derived, the essentially acephalous, segmentally structured society of the Bedouins as contrasted with the stratified, chief-oriented society of the Central Asiatic Turks.

One can, I think, now give a succinct answer to the question with which this inquiry began: while the almost total disregard of boundaries that characterized al-Idrisi's work is extreme, examination of the works of more than twenty Muslim geographers' writing over the period from 820 to 1320 AD shows that boundaries were indeed given little attention or were ignored altogether in the literature. The core and boundary zone hypothesis for describing any state appears to represent the underlying attitude adequately. Somewhat similar boundary concepts recur irregularly in other civilizations but the factors giving rise to the concept appear to differ markedly from one civilization to the next. As an example, one might note that the boundary zone concept characteristic of parts of the frontiers of Republican Rome was replaced by the idea of firm and largely defensive boundaries after Augustus' reign, and after Diocletian's reforms, boundaries reflecting in-depth defense replaced these.[173] Thus, interpretation of the social significance of the facts developed for the Islamic world will have to be deferred until more extensive comparative data are on hand.

---

[173] Cf. Dyson, S.L., *The Creation of the Roman Frontier* (Princeton, 1985); Parker, S.T., *Romans and Saracens* (Los Angeles, 1985); and Williams, S., *Diocletian and the Roman Recovery* (New York, 1985).

INDEX

[The transcription used to romanize Arabic terms throughout the text uses the Standard International Alphabet as employed, for instance, in H. Wehr's *Dictionary of Modern Written Arabic.* In the following Index the first recognizable Latin letter defines the letter under which the word is classified. Words beginning with ʿ or ʾ are shown at the end of the corresponding letter category-e.g. *ʿala* would be shown at the end of the entries beginning with 'a'; ḵums after kura.]

www.ingramcontent.com/pod-product-compliance
Lightning Source LLC
Chambersburg PA
CBHW050350110426
42812CB00008B/2422